Dot Calm

The Search for Sanity in a Wired World

Debra A. Dinnocenzo
Richard B. Swegan

16
EasyRead Large

RHYW

Copyright Page from the Original Book

Berrett-Koehler Publishers, Inc.
235 Montgomery Street, Suite 650
San Francisco, California 94104-2916
Tel: (415) 288-0260, Fax: (415) 362-2512
www.bkconnection.com

Ordering information for print editions
Quantity sales. Special discounts are available on quantity purchases by corporations, associations, and others. For details, contact the "Special Sales Department" at the Berrett-Koehler address above.
Individual sales. Berrett-Koehler publications are available through most bookstores. They can also be ordered directly from Berrett-Koehler: Tel: (800) 929-2929; Fax: (802) 864-7626; www.bkconnection.com
Orders for college textbook/course adoption use. Please contact Berrett-Koehler: Tel: (800) 929-2929; Fax: (802) 864-7626.
Orders by U.S. trade bookstores and wholesalers. Please contact Ingram Publisher Services, Tel: (800) 509-4887; Fax: (800) 838-1149; E-mail: customer .service@ingrampublisherservices.com; or visit www.ingrampublisherservices.com/ Ordering for details about electronic ordering.

First Edition
Paperback print edition ISBN 978-1-57675-152-7
PDF e-book ISBN 978-1-60509-821-0

2010-1

Designed by Detta Penna.
Cover design by Seventeenth Street Studio.

Set in 16 pt. Verdana

TABLE OF CONTENTS

To Thomas M'Clintock (1792–1876),
my great-great-great grandfather
and my hero
—R.S.

To Maria Mancini Caprara (1906–1994),
my grandmother, for her enduring wisdom
and legacy in my life
—D.D.

Foreword

We swing between extremes like the pendulum of a grandfather clock. At one end of the pendulum's arc, we see an exclamation point. At the other end, a question mark.

Swinging toward the exclamation point, we fling ourselves headlong into impossible work schedules fueled by fast food, motivational tapes and books on positive thinking. The idea is to win, to get ahead, to "unleash the giant within." But as the heady rush of adrenaline fades, we lose momentum and begin to fall back toward the question mark. Swinging past the center-point, we slip quietly into misty-eyed reflection about the meaning of life and start using words like *Zen.* The next step would be to shave our heads and start dancing in orange robes at the airport!

This book is for that reader who can hear the wind roar as the pendulum of their life swings wildly toward the exclamation point. Be of good cheer, gentle reader, for you'll find these pages to be filled with practical, how-to advice from the world's happiest and most successful executives—step-by-step formulas for finding your equilibrium, maintaining your symmetry and keeping balance in your life.

Things are about to get much better.

Read on.

Roy H. Williams
Williams Marketing, Inc.

www.wizardofads.com

Special Foreword

Why It's Good to Not Work Too Much

1. If you work too much on your computer, it might break down.

2. If you work too much, you may not get to spend enaugh time with your children.

3. If you talk on your cell phone too much, the batteries might run out.

4. If you work too much and make too much money, you might have to start another bank account to fit all the money in.

5. If you work too late at night, you might be tired in the morning.

Jennimarie Dinnocenzo Swegan
Age: 7

Preface

Dot Calm: The Search for Sanity in a Wired World will help you understand the realities of various forms of overload and guide you in your search for solutions to the problems created by overload. The overwired, frenzied, non-stop world in which we live impacts your life, your work, your health, and your relationships. We suspect, however, you need less help with understanding these realities (you're *living* them daily!) and more help on ways to handle them. Therefore, our main focus is on solutions to the problems created by overload, and on actions you can implement quickly and easily to make important changes in your life.

Our contributors provided many of the solutions and creative approaches we discuss here. The hundreds of people we surveyed or interviewed are probably much like you—overworked, tired, torn between conflicting priorities, and increasingly aware that something is missing in life. While many of the issues addressed are unique to the cultural dynamics of the U.S. society and workplace, the problems discussed can serve as a preview for those in other industrialized societies. Increasingly available and affordable technologies, increased access to information, and the globalization of electronic commerce will facilitate the transfer around the globe of opportunities—and problems—associated with a truly wired world. Therefore, readers beyond our shores can anticipate this reality and take steps to minimize negative consequences in their societies and their lives.

It is no coincidence that this book is in your hands (or on the screen of some electronic tool) at this particular moment. Whether you found it on a bookshelf or a website, received it as a gift from a concerned friend or loved one—or are lucky enough to have had it provided by an insightful employer—we trust that it has made its way to you because there's a need. And when there's a convergence of need, opportunity and information, wonderful things—and meaningful change—can occur. Therefore, we're delighted to be your guides on the path to greater calm, balance, focus, and congruence in your life and work. We can't think of a better way to invest our time or identify a more important contribution we can make to you, our readers—as well as your children, your communities, your organizations, and our society.

Thank you for reading our book, joining us on this important journey, and trusting that we can all find a better way to live and work.

Debra Dinnocenzo and Rick Swegan
Wexford, Pennsylvania, USA
2001

Acknowledgments

This book has been a labor of love for us—mostly because we still love each other after finishing it! While the end product is ours and we take responsibility for content, this book resulted from the input of more than two hundred people who completed questionnaires, provided reviews and critiques, participated in interviews, or engaged in lively discussions with us. While there are too many to mention by name, many of these people are named in the list of contributors to be found at the conclusion of the book.

We do want to thank some people specifically because without their efforts, this book would not have become a reality. The staff at Berrett-Koehler uncomplainingly answered our frequent questions and interjected doses of enthusiasm throughout this project. We are especially indebted to our editor, Steve Piersanti, for his vision, guidance, and support for our work. Detta Penna, our extraordinarily skilled production service and designer, has been a joy to work with and patient beyond words.

We offer abundant thanks to Roy Williams, the Wizard of Ads. Roy graciously agreed to provide the Foreword, as well as additional valuable ideas through his other writings. We appreciate his perspective, wit and incredible reliability.

Two people deserve our special thanks because, without them, we would never have finished. Janet Ruckel, our administrative assistant, provided her valuable time, editorial assistance, calm, and encouragement. Jenyce Woodruff, aspiring basketball star and truly fine young woman, provided untold hours of loving childcare that afforded us essential opportunities to write.

And last, but by no means least, we appreciate the contribution of our daughter, Jennimarie Dinnocenzo Swegan, whose enthusiasm, patience, humor, and love were key elements in our creative energy. We are also grateful for the contribution of her "stories" in the Special Foreword and Special Afterword. From the pens of babes—perspective and insight for us all!

Part One

Problem/Opportunity

It begins almost imperceptibly. A small voice within quietly whispers. Its persistence becomes somewhat familiar—a soothing sound that both nudges and nurtures. Words are not formed, though the feeling becomes clearer. And you slowly begin to understand. It is like a radio signal that is garbled by static, though the station is unquestionably transmitting. And as you travel forth, the static dissipates, the sounds emerge into words, and the small voice within is heard clearly:

Something Is Not Right!

This is the often slow and circuitous route by which you come to realize that your life is out of balance and that any semblance of control is only a distant memory, having long since been replaced by an overwhelming sense of O-V-E-R-L-O-A-D.

***

Throughout this book you will find sections set off by large quotation marks. These are direct quotes from respondents whose comments, provided via interview or survey, were especially relevant or poignant. We did not create any of these quotes. Each is an authentic—and sometimes instructive, provocative, or sad—statement from a real person. The authors are grateful to these contributors who offered such valuable insights, ideas, and wisdom.

***

This overload of information, communication, and the demands of work is beginning to take its toll. How often do you:

- Feel inundated by the volume and pace of information that relentlessly streams your way each day?
- Yearn for the days when taking a vacation meant that the office didn't travel with you?

> *"Access to information is so fast now that I try to get done as much as I can as fast as I can. Therefore, I try to put more on my plate because I can get it done quicker, which leads to more stress and shorter deadlines. Add in e-mail and having to manage that—and it can \cause havoc in your life."*

- Let phone calls interrupt precious time with family and wonder where to draw the line on the intrusion into your life that technology enables?
- Feel that "the faster I go, the behinder I get" as you satisfy the demand to operate at net speed,

while seeking the elusive work/life balance you so desperately desire?

- Wish you could simplify your life, slow your pace, feel more sane and balanced?

> *"I close the door to my office and leave it all behind. I focus on family. Work comes and goes, things come and go, but family is eternal. I am going to focus on the eternal things, because they are the important things. All this fuss we make about our livelihoods stops after we die. The family doesn't."*

- Feel the desire to be connected—not to networks or databases or message systems or wireless access, but to something deeper, higher, greater ... and to others?

WHAT TO DO? This is, of course, the operative question. While we can enumerate the virtues of technology and the myriad advantages we all enjoy as a result of nearly limitless access to information and communication resources, let's face it—most of us are exhausted, stressed out, frenetic, and oftentimes unfocused. Further, regardless of the technology tools we currently use to stay informed, connected, and tethered to our work, expect them to be replaced by newer, faster, and more intrusive tools aimed at increased productivity or accessibility. Improved technological tools and resources will not inherently minimize related problems without a conscious effort to manage the ways you deploy that technology in your work and life.

In the spirit of the simplicity everyone seems to crave, we have made every effort throughout this book to be efficient in the way information is provided and the ways you can access and apply it. Our hope is to transform the voice so that the calm, persistent message within you evolves to:

It Will Be All Right!

The wealth of ideas and solutions we have compiled were gathered through interviews, questionnaires, conversations, and e-mail messages involving people from a wide variety of jobs, industries, and career stages. From hundreds of sources, we have distilled the essence of their searching—the challenges, choices, and solutions for managing overload and achieving balance. So, as you read, bear in mind that we wrote according to the "rule of reality," recounting the struggles and successes shared with us by so many contributors. The stories are real, the frustrations authentic, and the solutions rooted in real-world questions that beg for answers. Out of these myriad suggestions and solutions, we trust you will find a kindred voice that speaks to your needs and offers solutions for which you, too, have been searching.

***

Everything should be made as simple as possible, but not simpler.

—Albert Einstein

1

Take Heed of Net Speed

Imagine a world where noise is everywhere. Not just surrounding you, but following you wherever you go. Some of that incessant clatter may be pleasant—bursts of music, laughter, sound of water. And some may be jarring—atonal, harsh, discordant. The constant din and jumble of sound seems to press on us, creating a brooding sense of tension, anxiety, and overload.

For most of us, this world doesn't really exist (although, as you walk through a busy city or a crowded airport, you may think so). If we substitute the image of noise for the reality of our daily lives, the accuracy of the image becomes clear. We live in an increasingly fast-paced, high-energy, constantly moving world where outside events intrude on our privacy and personal life. Everything around us shouts faster—faster connections, quicker service, and even faster fast food. No one is saying let's work more slowly and take our time. Whether you work in a "new economy" or "old economy" firm, run your own business, work in education, operate in the public sector, or attend school, the demands to make every minute count, to eke out every precious second for maximum multitasking, are constant. We now live in a 24/7 wired world bombarded by information that reaches us at lightning speed.

Prove the premise yourself. For a block of time, say, two weeks, notice how many articles, TV segments, radio spots, and advertisements address the issue of our increasing state of busyness. You'll be amazed by the results! We did a similar study and found:

> *"I carry an AA card, not because I drink, but because the 12 Steps remind me of the need to take one day at a time."*

- Articles in two weekly news magazines about children being overscheduled;
- A TV segment about the increasing number of business people who stay in touch with the office while on vacation;
- Articles about people disconnecting from their everyday work world;
- Several articles about rudeness associated with the use of cell phones;
- Countless articles about one aspect or another of Internet usage; and
- A variety of print ads and commercials targeted to those who are burdened by overload and/or those who seek more and faster connections.

These results provide a quick and compelling sense of the issues that are causing increasing discomfort for all of us.

Dot Calm: The Search for Sanity in a Wired World provides strategies for living and working well in the increasingly complex world in which we all live. We discuss both the speed and pace of our evolving e-world, and the serenity and calmness we all seek. The desire for calmness is a search—a journey that holds challenges, choices, and consequences. It is a never-ending process as each of us adjusts to new issues, challenges, and technologies.

The challenges we have faced, individually and as a couple, in efforts to balance the demands of work, relationships, family, and faith are also reflected in *Dot Calm: The Search for Sanity in a Wired World.* Our experience serves as a frame of reference for the gathering and retelling of the collective experience of others on a similar search.

Our research reveals there are three major trends that impact your life in today's highly connected world:

- **Access Overload**
- **Information Overload**
- **Work Overload**

What defines these types of Overload, how they've come to exist, and what you can do about them, comprise the major focus of this book. But, before proceeding with that discussion, let us offer a word of clarification. It would be easy to dismiss what we say as the ranting of anti-technology Luddites who yearn for the "good old days." However, that's clearly not the case. We own and use many of the technology tools available and discussed in this book. These tools provide us with numerous benefits, both in terms of our ability to stay in touch with others and to share information. In reality, neither of us invests energy yearning for a return to simpler times. We don't think that will happen. The world will continue moving faster, with more tools and more information streaming your way—in multiple forms and at faster rates. The real challenge and focus of your search is learning how to maintain your sanity, a sense of balance, and the essential points of nontechnological connectedness in this constantly evolving high-tech world.

Access Overload

The proliferation of technology tools—designed to keep us informed, connected, and accessible—is creating a growing sense of Access Overload that threatens the balance and serenity that we seek and need in our lives. The simple truth is that there's not only more information, communication, and knowledge being shared, but it's also reaching us via an expanding array of ever-present—and potentially always ON—technology tools.

Access Overload is probably best described by contrast. Think back to twenty or twenty-five years ago, when most of us lived without voice mail, cell phones, paging, answering machines, and call forwarding. What was our world like then? Certainly the pace was slower. You could not assume that someone received your message when you called. If they returned your call, there was no guarantee you would be available, thus starting the much-dreaded round of telephone tag. At the end of the day, you couldn't check messages unless you could speak directly to someone in your office. And you certainly couldn't return calls, because there was no one there to answer them. Spending an hour every evening listening and responding to voice mail messages simply did not occur. Certainly, people could and did work in the evening, but they weren't directly accessible, whether at home or on the road.

Then came the new technologies. While it was, in reality, a gradual process, it seems that almost over-night everyone was *connected,* in touch around the clock. Consider how quickly we've moved to a world that expects twenty-four-hour access and response. Think about the last time you had a complaint or a technical problem and couldn't reach a "live" customer service or technical support person when you needed help. Our guess is that you wanted assistance immediately, but not via a website or fax service. We all want help when the need arises, regardless of the hour showing on the clock. It seems that all of us, at times, want and expect a 24/7 world.

"The technology, although great, makes you almost too accessible. I find myself constantly

> *checking e-mail, voice mail, or forwarding my number to a cell phone, to make me accessible during time that I used to consider private or wind-down time. Since I spend a huge amount of my day on the Web, I get massive amounts of information. Lots of it gets filed for later review, and most of what I file is never looked at again."*

You may recall a time when you had to ask someone if they had a fax machine. Now, of course, a fax machine is standard (and, some suggest, a soon-to-be-outdated technology), and few business cards today are printed without a fax number. What's more, now we can fax to each other over the Internet, at airports, in hotel rooms, directly to computers, and at home. It follows that these exploding and expanding fax capabilities (and the inherent levels of access that result) are not unlike the expanding uses and impact of wireless phones.

Beware: The Learning Curves

While some emerging technologies may contribute to your sense of being overwhelmed, there are hidden aspects of technology that also contribute to this dynamic. Specifically, this has to do with the learning curve associated with any piece of new technology. While it can be as simple as a new voice mail system or as complex as a software program, it takes time to learn. Often it may take several hours or more to "get up to speed" on a single application. When you combine this with the number of mistakes that will naturally be made and the multiple systems (for example, a home voice mail, work voice mail, and cell phone voice mail) a person may be using, the learning curve itself may contribute to Overload.

***

Accessibility for emergencies, safety, or family connections has, of course, undeniable benefits. However, being accessible to others on a twenty-four-hour basis has, for many of us, led to Access Overload. Simply put, you can no longer escape. If you choose, you can be reachable anytime, anywhere in the world—and this takes a toll. Or, sometimes, we don't even choose it. Think back to the not-too-distant past when it was relatively rare to receive a business call at home. Given cell phones and pagers, many of us are reachable even when we don't want to be. Therefore, at least one part of Access Overload is the loss of privacy as technology has invaded our personal time and space. To a large degree, a home is no longer a "castle," because anyone can breach the walls electronically. Telemarketers who interrupt your evening are an all-too-constant reminder of this.

If you assume that the loss of privacy is one outcome of Access Overload, it is also realistic to suggest that time, as a boundary, has become meaningless. It is not that the clock on the wall no longer has meaning, or that we don't, to some extent, order our lives by it. Rather, it suggests that with a 24/7 mentality comes the reality that the eight-hour workday is now artificial. Not only do time zones cease to exist as a barrier to communication but also, as those walls have broken down, the premium on speed of response has gone up exponentially. We are more accessible in our own country and just as accessible to others around the world.

As a result, the eight-hour workday has become distorted, as has the workweek and the distinction between work and vacation. One direct result of Access Overload is the assumption on the part of some managers, customers, and coworkers that you will be accessible all the time, and that you'll use your personal time to stay connected. The fact that, for many people, there is literally no "down time" is creating a toll on relationships, families, and emotional well-being.

At its most basic level, Access Overload interferes with our ability to interact with others. Along with a rise in mobile phone use, there's been an increase in articles about the rudeness of cell phone users. More restaurants are now restricting cell phone usage just as they restrict smoking. Or on a more personal level, how many of us have had romantic evenings with significant others or family activities interrupted by cell phone calls and/or a beeping pager? Of course, some jobs require that people be accessible, due to the life-and-death nature of their jobs, and we're certainly not suggesting that on-call doctors and others in critical jobs turn off their pagers for the sake of romance! However, what constitutes URGENT has become redefined by technology that confuses urgency with *accessibility.*

For many of us, and our anecdotal data support this, high levels of access are overwhelming. While this book is not specifically about stress or stress management, it *is* stressful for many of us to live under the constant tyranny of access. The fear that something important might be missed, the desire to connect with others, and the simple anxiety created by a ringing phone may overwhelm some people. At a minimum, constant access, when combined with the other Overload factors, creates the very real sense that the world is moving ever faster and becoming more out of control.

> *"You have to stop imagining that, just because you have access everywhere, you need to use it."*

The Overload Response

Throughout this book, Overload issues are addressed, along with their effect on each of us. Clearly, the way each of us responds to Overload varies tremendously. Some of us, for example, crave access. We want and need to be connected, while others shrink from access and find it oppressive. And, while our individual response may vary based on a wide variety of factors, the effect of Access Overload has negative consequences for most of us.

***

There are certain business situations, of course, where work will be intense. Proposals must get out overnight, urgent projects must be completed, production crises demand our attention, or a host of other legitimate issues arise, creating intensive work situations for short periods of time. This is a reality of life. When, however, this is the constant state of the work environment, the cumulative impact of work, access, and information Overload becomes destructive.

Constant access can be daunting and, at a minimum, represents an invasion of our psychic space. When you add the avalanche of information to this equation, the burden placed on people to manage and control their lives becomes even more extreme.

Information Overload

The speed at which information is created and bombards us causes a pervasive sense of Information Overload. This accompanies an overwhelming, defeated feeling of being perpetually unable to process everything. While information, communication, and knowledge are being shared at a vastly greater rate than ever before, so many of us feel woefully incapable of handling it all. Even before the advent of the

Internet, most of us felt buried in data and information. Consider the media, for example. Where once there were three basic TV channels, now we have access to hundreds of channels. Multiple channels offer a dizzying array of programming—all news, all sports, movies, education, history, science, and the list goes on.

The same explosion of offerings extends to radio, magazines, and other printed media. To get a quick sense of this, just browse for twenty minutes in a mega bookstore. Stop at the magazine section and scan the range of titles and subject matter. Notice the number of magazines and/or topics that wouldn't or couldn't have existed ten years ago. If you want to feel even more overwhelmed, stop and look at the number of topic areas for books and the incredible number of books that exist in each area. Multiply the number of books in a bookstore by the number of new titles published each year (estimated to be as high as 150,000), and the colossal volume of available information becomes staggering.

Yet this describes the volume of information that surrounds us at only one level. Add to this the explosion of information created by the Internet, e-mail, and other wireless tools, the amount of information now available becomes mountainous!

The avalanche of information currently provided on the Internet is almost incomprehensible. It's estimated that more than 1.5 million pages are added to the Web each day, and that Internet use doubles every one hundred days. However, the Internet, in and of itself, is not the major culprit behind Information Overload. At the same time, the way we search the Internet and gain access to important information can contribute to overload.

> *"The proliferation of e-mail allows for immediate exchange of thoughts and attached data, which carries with it an expectation of immediate response. I find I am reviewing more information and data in one day than I used to see in a month. Many e-mails now carry links to websites, which then lead me to additional information, and so on."*

The real gremlin behind Information Overload is e-mail. While we are certainly users and advocates, e-mail clearly adds a different dynamic and a layer of complexity to Information Overload. As mentioned previously, e-mail is a major contributor to Access Overload. It is an even bigger contributor to Information Overload. Why? Here are a few reasons:

- It is very difficult to separate requests for information from the sharing of information. Certainly there are filtering systems available for most e-mail systems, but even the best don't stop the deluge of messages.
- e-Mail truly knows no time boundaries. Messages can be sent and received at all hours of the day. While this has many advantages, it is very easy to

face a situation where you have "emptied" your inbox at the end of the day only to find that it has filled with thirty or more messages by morning.

- Many e-mail messages include attachments, which can be voluminous in their own right.
- e-Mail grows exponentially. It is very easy in an e-mail system to copy several hundred of your "closest" friends or "most important" colleagues! Our experience tells us that as soon as someone does that, the responses begin to grow at a rapid geometric rate—not in response to the importance of the message, but simply because people now feel they are involved, need to be noticed or, in truth, really do have something to contribute.
- Just like voice mail, e-mail can serve as a substitute for face-to-face communication. Sometimes it's easier and more appropriate to dash off an e-mail message, particularly when sharing information. In some cases, though, e-mail can unleash confusion and misunderstanding that would not have been created by face-to-face or voice-to-voice discussion. Aside from the resulting controversy, such e-mail exchanges can result in increased time to resolve a problem.

Information Overload can lead us to feel frantic and out of control. Try as we might, the tyranny of e-mail is inescapable. Once we complained about processing volumes of paper from our overflowing in-baskets. Now those paper in-baskets have been replaced by e-mail. The significant difference is that e-mail can follow us *anywhere* and can arrive *anytime.* Unlike "snail" mail, which is dependent on certain delivery times and schedules, e-mail is timeless and inescapable.

At its worst e-mail can overwhelm us. We can shut it off to go on vacation or transmit auto-response "out-of-office" messages. However, the e-mail messages continue to accumulate. For many, the feeling is one of treading water. Simply to keep our head above water, we feel we must continually process e-mail just to keep from drowning. The impact can be exhausting.

> *"I can't put more hours on the clock! It is my belief that the person most likely to lie awake fretting and worrying at night is the one who feels the need to answer the phone every time it rings, return every phone call to everyone who leaves a message, and type a response to every e-mail. May the Lord have pity on that poor soul. Amen."*

While Access Overload may lead to an invasion of our psychic space, Information Overload adds a layer of frenzy to the mix. We seem to swim through an ocean of information, and the ocean keeps getting wider and deeper.

Work Overload

The never-ending sea of information and access results in a "wireless tether." We are constantly tied to the tools and information resources designed to free us and provide greater mobility, while subjecting legions of us to Work Overload. There is a growing sense, matched by a growing reality, that our work is always with us, following us wherever we go, demanding immediate attention and responses.

In Japan, it is estimated that over 10,000 people die annually from overwork, or *karoshi.* While karoshi is not a reportable cause of death in other countries, we need only look at the literature on stress to gain a quick sense that overwork is a major problem. Researchers from Australia, Canada, and Germany also connect overwork to heart disease and other illnesses. Articles appear frequently about overwork, as well as the sheer overscheduling of lives—including, as more people are pointing out, the overscheduling of our children. Many of us have seen others (or considered ourselves) dropping out to pursue something else, stepping off the fast track or in some other way changing lifestyles to a simpler or more meaningful choice.

Indeed, the whole "simplicity" movement can be seen as a response to Overload issues and the pace of life. Certainly, there are some similarities between that movement and our research. But we are addressing the problem with a different perspective and a different set of solutions.

> *"I don't have any effective strategies for balance. In fact, my work "time" commitment has expanded to such an extent that personal time is secondary to work time."*

What is happening? A variety of forces are converging to create the problem of Work Overload. What leads us to that conclusion is a number of trends, including:

- *More people report blurred lines between work and home.* All too often, people no longer feel they can separate themselves from work and, if they do, they risk falling behind. This is not only a daily work issue but it carries over into vacations, weekends, and other holidays. As a personal example, during the past five years we have not taken a vacation where one or both of us remained completely out of touch with the office. And it seems this is more typical of others, as well.
- *The very notion of the workday and workweek have come under siege.* With the possible exception of the thirty-five-hour workweeks legislated by some Western European countries, workdays and workweeks have gotten longer and less uniform. As Juliet Schor points out in *"The Over-*

worked American" (1993), most Americans are working the equivalent of at least an extra month every year. Further, the U.S. Department of Labor estimates that a significant number of Americans work 260 hours per year beyond the level created by the "normal" forty-hour workweek. A recent study by the International Labor Organization reveals that Americans annually work almost two weeks more than Japanese workers. The problem is described vividly and accurately by Alan Ehrenhalt *(USA Today,* January 3, 2001): "There isn't any official rest period. There's no longer an hour on the clock when you can legitimately say, 'Nobody in his right mind would still be working now.'"

- *The pressure to increase productivity and to do more with less remains constant.* In this age of downsizing and layoffs, the amount of work to be completed has not decreased. Rather, the same amount of work, or more, is expected of fewer people. Contrary to some views, we do not believe Work Overload is attributable solely to the fear of being downsized. People are working harder because they feel they have to in light of volumes of work, competitive cultures, performance expectations, or personal achievement goals. In some cases, the pressure to work longer hours is self-generated. People may be extending their workday as an escape from a problematic personal or home life, from a desire to feel important and needed, or to create an external sign of success.

- *Technology has presented us with the promise of increased freedom, time savings, and greater autonomy, but for many of us the promise seems hollow.* Productivity enhancement tools such as e-mail seem initially to provide the solution. Over time, however, they simply add another burden of complexity, pressure, and time demands.

> *"With phones and the Internet, you are always working when you leave the office. The work goes with you because you're always accessible."*

- *The promise of dot-com riches seduced many into the abyss of overwork.* The emptiness of that promise—and the unreasonableness of the trade-offs—is increasingly apparent.

The convergence of Access, Information, and Work Overload leaves many feeling suffocated. It's as though you are slowly sinking into a pool of quicksand, where the harder you struggle, the more you sink. Further, you believe you should have the ability to manage your burdens and reach some degree of balance in your daily life. In truth, the ability to avoid drowning in our overloaded, overwired world is indeed attainable. Developing this ability involves knowledge, skills, and perspectives that are addressed in the remaining sections of this book. Bear in mind, however, that the elusive search for perfect balance is a futile effort. As our research and experience suggest, a more reasonable objective is a *congruent* life that creates opportunities for balance.

An integrated or congruent life accepts the ebb and flow of demands and seeks the benefits technology affords us. The ability to work anywhere, anytime, allows us to mesh our work role and commitments with our personal objectives and obligations.

> *"I firmly intend, commit, and resolve to be the same person exhibiting the same core values and behavior when fulfilling each of my life roles. How do I do this? I don't pursue balance (a term that for me denotes scarcity) but instead I pursue integration. I strive to blend each part of me into each other part so that I am always a Dad, always a husband, always a writer, always a business man, always a whole person showing up. I consistently re-visit the foundational philosophy that I first authored about twelve years ago. It describes my life purpose, vision, current mission, and guiding principles. If I change, I change that philosophy."*

Regardless of the semantics used or the specific ways you reconcile competing demands for your time and attention, one fundamental truth exists: **The choice is yours.** All of the pressures, demands, expectations, and requirements you experience in our evolving, wired world can only affect your time, energy, accessibility, and work/life balance to the degree that you choose. And, like so many other life choices, you must consider the consequences and tradeoffs that impact your job, career, family, relationships, health, and quality of life. The personal values underlying your choices are best expressed if clearly understood and consciously applied throughout your life. Herein lies your true search for both sanity and a congruent life.

***

It's not the pace of life that concerns me.
It's the sudden stop at the end.

—Seen on a T-shirt

2

Launch the Search Engine Within

Most of us are affected by the frenetic changes that have occurred in our world over the last decade. This chapter is designed to help you assess, through self-diagnosis, how these changes impact your life. If you know you are overwhelmed and know why, you might want to move on. The remainder of this book addresses solutions and actions to help you get your Overload situation under control.

This chapter includes a series of short exercises and self-assessments (printable versions are available at www.dotcalmbook.com) designed to diagnose problems or concerns created by Overload. As you proceed, please keep the following in mind:

- There are no right or wrong answers. This is rooted in the philosophy that your personal insights are more meaningful than scores on a scale.
- While this section is based on a self-assessment approach, additional perspectives may sometimes be in order. Therefore, it may be very important and revealing occasionally to check your perceptions with someone else. Ask your spouse, a friend, a business associate, or someone close to you to provide feedback on some of the self-diagnostic

areas. Another approach is to ask someone to interview you using the tools and questions that follow.

- The process begins with a set of foundational questions. These are followed by a series of more penetrating activities that further elaborate on each question.

The Keystone Questions

1. *What do I value most in life? What's most important to me? What am I passionate about?*
   [Space left intentionally blank in the original book]
2. *Is the way I spend my day or week consistent with the above? Where do I really spend my time?*
   [Space left intentionally blank in the original book]
3. *Am I feeling overworked? Under pressure? What is my state of mind relative to balance, or the lack thereof, in my life?*
   [Space left intentionally blank in the original book]
4. *To what degree am I tethered to the various productivity tools I use (voice mail, e-mail, PDA or personal digital assistant, cell phone)? How essential are these tools to my ability to live and work well?*
   [Space left intentionally blank in the original book]
5. *Am I in control of my life—or is it controlling me? Why?*
   [Space left intentionally blank in the original book]

***

As mentioned earlier, we strongly believe in the value of feedback from others to help ground our perspective in reality. Complete the Keystone Questions and then use them to interview your spouse or significant other about your behavior.

As discussed in Chapter 1, balance is a function of choice. Your choices are based on what you value or what is truly important to you at a core level. Our suspicion is that too many people either don't consciously examine their values or make choices based upon them. Use the following exercise to help you to explore and define your values.

The Value Questions

Take some time to think about your answers to the following questions. Write your answers in this book or document them in another way. Writing your responses encourages greater reflection and commitment to your answers.

1. *If I asked others to describe me, what would they say? Do I want them to describe accomplishments, relationships, and/or some other aspect of my life?*

[Space left intentionally blank in the original book]

2. *What are the five most important things in my life? How do I prioritize them?*

[Space left intentionally blank in the original book]

3. *What are the objectives, or goals, for my life?*

[Space left intentionally blank in the original book]

4. *How do I measure success?*

[Space left intentionally blank in the original book]

5. *When I look back on my life, of what am I proudest? Of what am I not proud?*

[Space left intentionally blank in the original book]

6. *What is my greatest achievement? Why?*

[Space left intentionally blank in the original book]

7. *What is the best decision I've made in my life? Why?*

[Space left intentionally blank in the original book]

***

Assuming you either know what you value or have gained greater clarity, the question becomes "Now what?" The central issue is congruence between your values and your actions. In his book, *Integrity* (1996), Stephen Carter defines integrity as "discerning what is right and what is wrong; acting on what you have discerned, even at personal cost; and saying openly that you are acting on your understanding of right and wrong." We believe that congruence is:

- Knowing what values are important to you.
- Acting on those values, even at personal cost.

- Stating openly the values on which you are acting.

Congruence is important for a variety of reasons. To act congruently means making conscious choices; it links actions to priorities; and it creates an awareness that integrates and connects.

> *"I've chosen an economic lifestyle that doesn't need the high-end support that many of my peers have. I've reduced my expenses by limiting my "wants." The technique is "to choose.""*

To look further at the issue of congruence, it's essential to combine analysis of your values with how you actually act. The following Time Question exercise will help you with this process.

The Time Questions

Directions: Estimate the percentage of time you spend in the following activities each week. (If you want a more accurate estimate, refer to your calendar or PDA. You might also track your activities in detail for a week to provide even greater accuracy.) Not all of the items may apply to you, so ignore those that aren't relevant or add others that are applicable.

1. Travel to or from work ______
2. Additional work-related travel ______

3. Work ______
4. Socialize with friends ______
5. Spend time with your family ______
6. Community activities ______
7. Entertainment ______
8. Sleep ______
9. Spiritual endeavors ______
10. Exercise ______
11. Relaxation ______
12. Education/Self development ______
13. ______ ______
14. ______ ______
15. ______ ______

Take a few minutes to examine the percentages. This is not a time to fool yourself with erroneous figures, so review your entries for accuracy. (This might also be a good point for a reality check with a significant other.) The key here is to examine the congruence between what you say you value and where you really spend your time. Another way to gain added insights is to review the list, prioritizing the items from most important to least important. Do your priorities match with the ways that you spend your time?

***

The focus has been on acquiring greater awareness of how choice plays out in your personal life *and* how you bring your values and actions together to function effectively. There is a flip side to all this—when the burdens of living with the various forms of Overload become overwhelming and create dysfunction.

You'll recall the previous mention of *karoshi,* or death by overwork. There is ample evidence that stress or burnout does take a significant toll on workers of all ages. The American Institute of Stress (www.stress.org) reports on research conducted over the past two decades that reveals:

> *"When I get asked to join groups/organizations, or get asked to chair certain projects within those groups, I always assess the opportunities against my Value Principles, which I define every year. I then look to see if the opportunity that is presenting itself fits with where I want to be, who I want to be, and with future knowledge in a particular area."*

- Forty-three percent of all adults suffer adverse effects due to stress.
- Stress has been linked to all the leading causes of death, including heart disease, cancer, lung ailments, accidents, cirrhosis, and suicide.
- Nearly half of all American workers suffer from symptoms of burnout, a disabling reaction to stress on the job.
- Sixty to eighty percent of industrial accidents are due to stress.

For some of us, Access Overload, Information Overload, and Work Overload make a major contribution to stress in our lives. If you think you are reacting to stress physically, mentally, or emotionally, read on. If that's not the case for you, consider skipping this section.

***

Stress

As defined by www.accenthealth.com, "stress is the way you react physically, mentally, and emotionally to various conditions, changes, and demands in your life." Each of us responds to stress differently. Some of us embrace it and use the force of it to drive our actions—in short, it is a motivator. For others, stress can be a huge negative—leading to ulcers, panic attacks, or worse. There are many good resources on stress and stress management, many of which are accessible on the Internet. The following list includes some signs of stress. If you experience any of these, consider further exploration of the causes and implications of your stress, as well as techniques for managing the negative impact of it in your life. Typical signs of stress include:

- Frequent headaches
- Difficulty sleeping
- Irritability
- Depression

- Continual exhaustion
- Edginess
- Forgetfulness
- Negative feelings
- Concentration difficulties
- Inability to relax

While these symptoms may be stress-induced, they may also have some physical cause. Therefore, if you persistently exhibit any of these symptoms, we strongly recommend you consult a physician.

***

People juggle a variety of technology tools to manage their work and their world. Many of us have multiple e-mail accounts, several voice mail accounts, and a number of passwords to help us manage. The issue is complicated to a further level by the number of times a day such tools are accessed. Almost everyone we questioned referred to the amount of time it takes to process e-mail and voice mail—time that used to be set aside for different activities.

Fifty years ago, only bridges were stressed. *Humans were nervous, worried or fearful. Since the 1950s, stress has evolved* *from an engineering term to a cultural construct.*

New Media Workshop
Columbia University Graduate
School of Journalism
http://stress.jrn.columbia.edu/

The tools you use to manage access and information, plus the frequency with which you use them may, in fact, contribute to Overload. To some extent, many of us may be approaching a catch-22, where the tools we use to solve the problem have become part of the problem. To assess this for yourself, complete the exercise on pages 29 and 30.

Your Use of Technology Tools

As you complete the following survey, include both business and personal tools.

1. How many voice mail systems do you maintain?

a. Business ______
b. Cell Phone ______
c. Home ______
d. Other ______

2. How often do you access your voice mail(s) each day?

a. Business _____

b. Cell Phone _____

c. Home _____

d. Other _____

3. Do you carry a pager? Yes _____ No _____
More than one pager? Yes _____ No _____

4. How many e-mail boxes/systems do you maintain?

a. Business _____

b. Home _____

c. Other _____

5. How often do you check e-mail?
Once a day _____ Twice a day _____
Three times a day _____ Four/more times a day _____

6. Do you carry a PDA or some other form of time management system? Yes _____ No _____
How many? _____

7. How often do you check messages?

a. e-Mail _____ _____

b. Voice mail _____ _____

c. Other _____ _____

In reviewing your responses (since there is no correct standard applicable to everyone), consider if your use of and access to technology tools is the appropriate level for you. Some of us may use a variety of tools infrequently, while others have a few tools that are used constantly. Most of us fall somewhere between the extremes. What's right for you is determined by what feels appropriate, supports your values, and fulfills your vision; helps you effectively and efficiently achieve personal and work-related goals; and represents a tolerable level of intrusion into your life.

True Confessions

Just so you don't think we're saints about all of this, we completed the Tools survey ourselves. Bearing in mind that we maintain a home-based business and one of us has a corporate job, here is a brief overview. Between us we maintain: seven business-related voice mailboxes, two cell phones, and three mailboxes on our home phone. In addition, coming into our home we have at least four voice lines (not including the three identifying-ring numbers on our home phone), two dedicated fax lines and a high-speed access line. Each of us carries a PDA, and between us we maintain eight different e-mail boxes.

Focusing on accessibility, the issue becomes even more complex. Most of the time, because we are parents, one or more of our phone lines is forwarded to a cell phone. This is almost always true if we are away from home or expecting a call.

Relative to how often our various systems are accessed, we are almost polar opposites. One of us accesses his various systems on average twice a day. The other accesses her systems an average of four or more times a day and almost always, including weekends, ends the day by checking her systems (every last one of them)!

Naturally, the Tools survey is helping us reexamine our approach to staying connected and reevaluate our levels of access. We are exploring integrated telephone/message systems and one-number access options. Additionally, we have cancelled our pager service and curtailed the dissemination of our cell phone numbers (don't look for them at the end of this book!).

***

It's clear that being successful with your life—as opposed to being successful in life—is a function of living a congruent life. This involves bringing your values to consciousness *and* making choices consistent with your critical values. Your age, career stage, and life changes will necessitate adjustments and new choices as time goes on. The process of living a congruent life is not static; it is a dynamic process requiring constant fine-tuning. The search for congruence and sanity is a journey that mandates continued changes in direction.

***

In the middle of the road of my life I awoke in a dark wood Where the true way was wholly lost.

—*Dante Alighieri,* The Commedia

3

How Organizations Help and Hinder

The organizations most of us work for, support, or create are driven by the increasing demand to operate at net speed. Nothing can be done fast enough. Fear of falling behind or not being first to market is an obsession, and the expectation or need to operate in a 24/7 mode is pervasive. Indeed, it is a competitive mandate to go ever faster. Many organizations deploy extensive technology resources and solutions that enable a wired workforce to establish digital connections around the globe. Concurrently, expectations for productivity improvements continue to increase.

> *"My organization does strive for balance as an ultimate idea, but realizes we aren't there right now and won't be in the near future. I got calls at the hospital while I was having my baby. Need I say more?"*

As a result, a dichotomy often exists between organizational needs and expectations in the age of technology and the struggle for balance and sanity at an individual level. Individuals are being pushed to do more at a faster pace by their organizations—and the organization continues to raise its expectations as new productivity tools and processes are developed. The conflict between individual choices and organizational demands must be reconciled to ensure the success both of the organizations and the people that comprise them.

***

The Evolution of Intrusion

If you've been in the workforce for a decade or so, you'll recall that in the not-too-distant past there was a greater sense of respect for the separation of one's work and personal worlds. A different standard operated in terms of justifiable intrusion into someone's personal time. It was perceived as far more unseemly a decade ago, for example, to call someone at home in the evening or on the weekend—or on vacation, for sure!—about a work issue. There were certainly exceptions, and we can recall more than a few occasions of this ourselves. However, as a general rule, work interruptions during personal time occurred far less often than today.

What has led to this significant escalation in interruptions to our personal time? The evidence points to the proliferation of technology tools that enable us to be so much more accessible. Certainly the availability of sophisticated, two-way pagers and wireless e-mail systems facilitate this reality. Also, the common use of cell phones and the "always on" impression they create has contributed significantly to this dynamic. Some people perceive it to be less intrusive if they call someone during the weekend on their cell phone rather than on their home phone. And indeed, there's a greater likelihood of a connection, because so many of us feel compelled to keep our cell phones with us and turned on almost all the time. We need to look at the degree of intrusion this creates in our lives. Think about this the next time you're at a Little League game or school soccer match. How many parents are watching their kids play while taking calls on their cell phones from work associates who don't think they're really interrupting? Even if the parents don't mind the interruptions, how do you suppose the kids feel?

Organizations—corporate, service, and entrepreneurial environments alike—are beginning to realize that doing more and doing it faster does not necessarily equate with doing the RIGHT things that get the RIGHT results. In the haze of our frenzied, high-tech, Web-enabled work world, it's beginning to dawn on many of us that there may be a more effective way to achieve results and manage our work. The truth is, it is now critical to focus in ways that haven't been necessary in the past.

Focus, Focus, Focus

Focus can be achieved when people know what they're doing, why they are doing it, how they should do it, and how their results will be rewarded. Few of us question the value of focus. The plethora of successful books that aim to get us on the right path—employing the most effective habits, using the most productive work and success techniques, and setting clear goals—provide resounding evidence of the importance of focus.

> *"We are accustomed to measuring work in terms of productivity (end results) not just activity (seeing how busy you are). Because we have a great deal of clarity around both purpose and priorities, it is fairly easy to make sure that what we are doing individually meshes with the overall goals of the company. This, in and of itself, greatly supports our focus."*

Successful organizations—those that achieve results or exceed expectations, however those metrics are quantified—always begin by clearly articulating goals. Organizational goals are driven through the business planning process and are expressed in measurable, identifiable, and achievable goals at the business unit, team, and individual level. This means that each person in the organization should know:

- Why their job exists.
- What their function contributes to the overall business plan and objectives.
- Why their contribution is valuable.
- How they should achieve their goals.
- How their results will be measured and rewarded.

> *"It's very helpful to have the focus, as well as the vision, values, and critical success factors, provided by a performance management system."*

Consider the flip side, something with which many of us have entirely too much experience. Without clear expectations, people begin to feel—and indeed are—unfocused, frustrated, and angry. They invest time and energy in what they *think* is the right thing to do, with little assurance that this is consistent with what's important to the organization. In the absence of focus, and with the vast amount of information, input, and interruptions bombarding people, there's a natural tendency to respond to whatever seems to be urgent at the moment, regardless of its true importance. As a result, you may feel compelled to thoroughly read, listen to, and respond to every one of the 95 e-mails, 35 voice mails, and 10 faxes you receive in a typical day. How, you wonder, is this really possible, in light of the meetings, routine work, interruptions, and phone calls that must also fit into your day? Not to mention that you have and want a life outside of work!

> *"There is only so much we can assimilate and apply day-to-day. Information comes in the form of mail, e-mail, newspapers, magazines, television, radio, Internet, telephone calls, and in-basket. It can really overwhelm you. The other over-load I experience is Access Overload. Clients, friends, and family want you to be accessible around the clock via e-mail, cellular phone, and regular phone."*

The expanding array of technology tools available to us drastically increases the rate at which information, messages, and other demands for our attention bombard us. Because access can easily be confused with urgency, there's often a tendency to respond immediately to things that drop into our various virtual in-boxes. This is clearly a problem for anyone not focused on a set of priorities that is tied to business imperatives. It is also a problem for those working in organizations that don't have clear protocols regarding the use of communication tools. There's an even bigger problem for people in organizations that have a culture that encourages or expects near-instant responses to messages.

"People want to access you and your brain 24 hours a day, and when they can't have it, many become annoyed."

e-Communication Culture

In our consulting with organizations that are establishing or expanding their remote work programs, we often discuss the need for clearly articulating an e-communication culture. This means raising awareness and increasing sensitivity to the communication needs of geographically dispersed associates and global teams. Further, it involves increased cognizance of the importance of using e-mail, fax, voice mail, or Intranet capabilities to share information and keep remote workers in the communication loop, regardless of the location or time zone in which they work.

"people in our company perceive that sending an e-mail is a substitute for real communication. One colleague has actually said to me, "We talked about that yesterday," when in reality he only had sent me several e-mails yesterday. I think e-mail is fine, but I don't want people to think that we've "talked" when we've only exchanged digital messages."

An effective e-communication culture includes a defined set of expectations as to how various information and communication tools will be used. For example:

- Will e-mail be used for routine communication, while voice mail is the standard for more urgent communication?
- When is it appropriate to page people?
- What constitutes an acceptable use of cell phones?
- What types of information should be communicated by voice mail?
- What voice mail standards should be utilized in both mailbox greetings and messages transmitted?
- What types of information should be communicated by fax?
- Are there volume and size limits on the documents attached to e-mail?
- When should spreadsheets, slide presentations, and multi-media resources be used to share information?
- When should the Intranet, shared drives, or file transfer sites be used?
- What are appropriate methods for filtering information and messages?

"I hate hearing that some critical information I need is available on our Intranet. I don't have

> *time to constantly check for new information. How am I supposed to know it's there, know where to find it, and have it available when Ineed it?"*

- How often are associates expected to access the various message and information sources?
- What response time frames are considered the norm?

Michael Schrage (*Fortune,* December 18, 2000) observes "The problem is not that these are difficult questions to answer but that they are so seldom asked." It's not reasonable for organizations to invest significant energy in attempting to control or legislate communication. However, organizations will benefit greatly—as will those who toil there—if expectations are clear regarding the use of communication and information resources. Without basic guidelines and clear expectations—driven by a fundamental focus on what's important to the organization—people tend to lose sight of priorities and begin to function as though everything demanding their attention is of equal importance and urgency. Schrage goes on to say "Companies that care about the value of people's time will invest as much effort in designing the technological rules of engagements as they do in the technology itself. In this era of rising choice, the ability to say no can be even more empowering than a willingness to say yes."

Adding to the demands and complexity of our modern work-world is the evolving meaning of work in our lives. While people seem increasingly aware that work does not represent ultimate meaning in their lives, work consumes an increasing amount of our time and energy. It seems that the quest for increased recreation and balance—and the promise offered by so many timesaving, productivity-enhancing technology tools—is an undisputed myth. As mentioned earlier, the average number of hours typically spent working each week is actually on the rise.

Naturally, most organizations will happily capitalize on this evolving workplace dynamic. What organization isn't being squeezed to do more with less, while stretching people to the limits of their time and capabilities? Which leaders secretly shudder at the thought of encouraging greater balance for their people, possibly resulting in fewer hours each week devoted to the work of the organization? Even those organizations that have explicit corporate values that support balance and encourage quality of life are often perceived to reward and reinforce behaviors that fly in the face of these values.

While those who work independently or on a contract basis may feel unsupported in their efforts to lead a balanced life, how many full-time employees in organizations experience similar feelings?

What are the implications to organizations that don't understand the importance of balance and don't nurture values that support focused priorities? As we've already discussed, organizations suffer greatly from the disconnect between critical business goals and the work that's accomplished. In their frenzied effort to do *everything*—a veritable impossibility—it's very likely that many of the *right* things are not accomplished.

> *"I am a freelance reporter, so the organizations I work for vary. None of them care about my achieving focus or balance. They just want me to achieve a story and send it to them."*

Beyond the frustration, anger, and exhaustion this causes, people tend to feel unappreciated and demoralized. Many of them reported to us that their organizations multiply their personal and professional burdens by consistently:

- Setting unrealistic timelines

> *"From the day I started with my company, I outlined for them the importance and order of my life. I have only had one manager who didn't respect and support that. I immediately looked for and received a different assignment to separate myself from that manager. Because I have stayed focused on what's important to me and demonstrated that*

I am a performer, I have more support than I ever dreamed possible."

- Establishing unattainable goals
- Giving only lip service to balance and quality-of-life issues
- Assuming or expecting a seven-day workweek
- Encouraging or requiring weekend meetings or teleconferences
- Expecting e-mail to be checked on weekends

So, where does this leave you if you work in a bonafide 24/7 environment that must function at net speed? How does an organization with a bias for action and results reconcile the need for speed with the demand for balance and sanity?

Our company does several things to help keep lives and work in balance:

• Forty-hour workweeks. This means devoting enough resources to a project so that people don't have to work beyond 40 hours per week.

• Take vacations. Our policy is, use them or lose them. As a result, people actually take their vacation weeks.

• Variety. We encourage different types of assignments and work to provide variety.

• Avoid time wasters. We minimize wasted time by not holding unnecessary meetings and by provid-

ing the technical support to help solve problems quickly.

How can organizations work collaboratively to ensure attainment of results (revenue, market share, growth, profit, shareholder value) while nurturing a value-driven work environment that protects the individual rights of privacy, personal time, and purpose? Those organizations successfully balancing these potentially conflicting demands are described by their employees as doing the following things the right way:

- Encourage people to be balanced.
- Convey a sense of awareness and understanding of the struggle for balance.
- Support flexible work arrangements, such as:

"My organization demands hard work but encourages adequate rest. They encourage times of training, input, rest, retreat if needed. They allow me to escape by not bothering me on my days off unless urgent things crop up. I am not micro-managed, therefore I have the liberty to manage my own life/schedule."

- Self-determined start/end times for the workday
- Company-supplied notebook computers

- Telecommuting
- High-speed network access from home
- Flextime
- Staggered start/end times
- Friday afternoons off in the summer
- Personal days
- Liberal vacation entitlement
- Family leave
- Alternate work schedules

• Empower employees to be self-managed.
• Place a sincere value on family time and commitments.
• Support and encourage short meetings.
• Support virtual work arrangements.
• Encourage people to leave at the end of their workday.
• Extend the holiday break in December.

In light of the extraordinary demands placed on organizations in our current marketplace, the recruitment and retention of highly skilled and highly motivated workers is essential to success. Wise organizations will further their prosperity by creating environments that support and nurture both the values of individuals and their ability effectively to integrate their personal lives with workplace demands. The absence of such a commitment—and translation of that commitment into action—on the part of organizations leaves them vulnerable to the loss of human capital.

"I left the organizational world because organizations are typically greedy institutions that will eat up as much of a person's time as possible."

***

Where there is no vision, the people perish

—Proverbs 29:18

Part Two

SOLUTIONS

The chapters in this section detail a wide variety of solutions that many people have employed to:

- Achieve balance
- Handle the various forms of Overload
- Manage accessibility
- Reconnect with themselves and others
- Establish priorities

Based on our research, we have identified five essential solutions that summarize the myriad of techniques and specific actions people can employ. These five essential solutions are:

1. Prioritize and organize.
2. Take daily time-outs.
3. Take mini-sabbaticals.
4. Nurture the soul and mind.
5. Nourish the body.

Beyond the essential solutions, there is a fundamental truth that governs all of the efforts to achieve your desired level of balance, calm, sanity, and satisfaction. To put it simply (and perhaps boldly), the degree of overload, overaccess, and overwork that exists in your life *were not inflicted upon you.* Rather, it's a reality that you've chosen to allow, accept or accommodate. Inherent in your choice, whether you're conscious of it or not, is an expression of your values and priorities.

Look Out the Other Window

At lunch on Sunday, our good friend Akintunde was saying that he hadn't been able to unwind for several weeks because he couldn't get his mind off of his troubles and the deadlines at work. (Akintunde is programming a new video game for Nintendo and the game keeps inexplicably crashing.) He looked at me and asked, "So how do you do it?"

Pointing to the east, I said, "Look out that window and tell me what you see." Akintunde looked carefully out the window and described in detail what he saw there. "Now look out this window," I said, pointing to the west, "and tell me what you see." Akintunde spent the next several moments describing an entirely different scene. I said, "That's how I do it." When he didn't understand, I pointed one last time to a bare wall and said, "Tell me what you see." Akintunde said "I see nothing but a blank wall." "Keep looking," I told him. After a minute of watching him stare silently at the wall, I asked, "Are you thinking about what you saw out the window?" "Yes, I am," he laughed, "How did you know?"

"Akintunde," I said, "If you will pour yourself into something that will occupy your evenings and weekends as completely as your job occupies 9 to 5, you will find that you will soon be feeling less tired, frustrated, and stressed about what is happening at the office." Akintunde looked like a man who had just been given permission to live. "I'm going to study grackles!" he shouted. "I've really been wanting to, but I thought it would just make me more tired." "Study grackles," we told him. Pennie and I fully expect Akintunde to become the world's foremost authority on grackles.

Like most people, our friend Akintunde had been confusing rest with idleness. Rest is not idleness. Rest is simply looking out a different window. If you have a job, or anything else that you struggle with and worry about, you have a window that looks to the east.

But do you have one that looks to the west?

Roy H. Williams
www.WizardofAds.com

4

The Connection Conundrum

Based on our research, there appears to be a growing backlash against the tyranny of 24/7 accessibility. With the exception of a handful of people who say, "I don't" in response to the question of how they limit accessibility, the majority of our research responses indicate people do limit, or try to limit, their accessibility to others. We describe this as a backlash because more than three-quarters of our contributors report their action to limit accessibility is a recent change for them. The exception to this seems to exist at very high levels of the organization, where people feel the need to be accessible constantly. Even at that level, however, there are many who try to limit access based on personal beliefs and values, or because they feel the need to model the behavior for the rest of the organization.

> *"I do not initiate or set up meetings, conference calls, etc., with people on evenings or weekends, and I discourage people from doing so. I try to model balance and reinforce balance. I leverage my travel time and do my late night paperwork, e-mail, and phone calls while I'm on the road."*

Given the rapid increase in the number of cell phones, pagers, notebook computers, PDAs, and other communication devices, each of us has to decide if and where a line will be drawn. As discussed in Chapter 1, people have become extremely sensitive to the perception that their psychic space is being invaded. This seems to be driving the backlash against excessive connectivity and access. A surprising number of our respondents mentioned that they physically go someplace where access is difficult in order to truly limit access to or from the rest of the world. Of course, a less drastic alternative is to stay where you are reachable, but choose to turn off those access tools!

Clearly, as much as you might try to escape access, it will increasingly follow you. Those oases once used for escape—remote cabins, cruises, wilderness treks—are steadily being invaded by technology. It appears to us that it will be a very short time before the whole world is connected at some level and that true escape from the "e-tether" becomes extremely difficult.

> *"I went on a cruise recently and the newest concept was on-board e-mail access. How can anyone who wants to get away for some relaxation time feel the need to stay connected on the Internet? Sure enough—I'd walk down for dinner and the ter-*

minals would be full of people (with a line) waiting to check e-mail!"

It's also clear that many people utilize a dual strategy to minimize access. A number of people describe a one-time event—a vacation, a trip, or some other form of escape. The implication is that evading accessibility is an occasional activity and that, during the rest of the year, around-the-clock accessibility is acceptable. While this approach may work every now and then, the real challenge is managing access on a day-to-day basis. Using short disconnect breaks to recharge and recapture your sanity allows you to return to the daily world refreshed. How you survive, though, is ultimately dependent on your ability to manage the daily grind.

So, how do people manage the daily demand of accessibility? Our research reveals two groups with distinct approaches. The first group, Technology Deployers, consists of those who believe that better and more effective use of technology will allow them to manage access. The second group, Technology Restrictors, is populated by those who control access by limiting their use of technology.

"Walking out the door each night, I make peace with my decision to quit for the day by saying to myself, "Let worlds collide, let millions die. I've

done all that I can." The next day when I arrive at the office and find that planets did not collide and millions did not die as a result of my having left a few things undone the previous day, I happily get back to work."

"Give Me More"—The Technology Deployers

The Technology Deployers believe that the solution to their access problem (and they do believe it is a problem) lies in the better use of technology or, in some cases, the anticipation that technology will improve and solve the problem. Our suspicion is that this group is the first to rush out and buy or adopt new technology, under the supposition that the latest and greatest gadget will make them faster and more effective, providing a competitive advantage.

From telephone technology to wireless e-mail capabilities, the Technology Deployers believe that, while they may be more accessible than they would like, the intrusiveness can be managed by processing it more quickly. The Technology Deployers also delegate to others more readily to help manage their accessibility. For example, number of the Technology Deployers are also high-level executives, the group that most often feels they have to be accessible. While this group tends to place a heavy reliance on technology, they also will make extensive use of assistants to help them monitor and control access.

"I make good use of all the available telephone technology: call waiting, call forwarding, answering machines, etc. I use caller ID to screen calls and only answer those I want to."

"While I check e-mail and voice mail every night before I go to bed, and over the weekend, I scan through them quickly by reading only the subject line or the first fifteen seconds of a message. I only respond to those that I think are urgent. I also filter e-mail so I only receive messages from my boss."

"Give Me Less"—The Technology Restrictors

While some people manage access through the use of technology, they are probably in the minority. Those in the larger group, the Technology Restrictors, manage their access by limiting the use of technology. That's not to say they don't use technology. Rather, they limit how much and when they will use it. This group, which appears to be growing, tends to operate with a mindset that dictates "Leave it in the desk, turn it off, don't give it out, and don't respond." Technology Restrictors are very clear about what they will and will not do. What they will not do is allow technology to create intrusions into their personal lives.

At the extreme, some Technology Restrictors are pointedly rebelling by discarding their cell phones, pagers, and answering machines. At its simplest, they don't purchase them in the first place. These people have clearly had too much and, in more extreme cases, are refusing to answer their phones or are living in homes without electricity to further remove themselves from the access barrage.

The more limited response, short of throwing technology away, moves control of access into the hands of the recipient. These people are the ones who selectively disclose their cell phone number or turn off their cell phone at a designated time. These are also the people who tend to turn off pagers or refuse to carry them (unless, of course, their job involves life-and-death situations or includes on-call requirements). Indeed, of all the technology tools mentioned by our survey respondents, pagers created the most emotional response. Either people use them extensively or they despise them and refuse to carry them. Pagers are perceived to be the most invasive of all the technologies currently used, and many people feel that pagers are an unreasonable invasion of their privacy.

> "I don't own a cell phone! I won't have a pager! Reason: In the business world no one really has to talk to you NOW. An hour from now or tomorrow is usually good enough. They would LIKE to talk to you NOW because they are ready NOW. You are probably not. Are you more productive working on YOUR schedule or theirs? If you allow 10–15 people to make their schedule your schedule, you will get little else done and will go quietly in sane!!! I believe this applies to work time as well as personal time."

While there appears to be little difference in the two groups in terms of the technology they use, the Technology Restrictors are quite clear in both their skepticism about technology and their unwillingness to let it drive their behavior. This is true both in their use of cell phones, voice mail, and pagers, as well as their use of e-mail. This is the same group that, by and large, refuses to access e-mail over the weekend and doesn't access e-mail or voice mail on vacations. Technology Restrictors seem to believe that if they plan appropriately, access is less of an issue and they will be contacted only in the event of a true emergency.

Setting Clear Expectations as a Way of Limiting Access

A theme that is supported by both Technology Deployers and Technology Restrictors is one that suggests you can control access by setting clear expectations for others. If people understand how you like to operate, they will respect those limits and be less willing to track you down with messages and pleas for responses that are not truly urgent.

> *"I always do voice mail at the end of the day and people know that—so they knowthat if they want a voice mail response, it had better be in there before 6:30p.m. or so."*

Those people who set expectations control access by being very clear about what they will do and when they will or won't be accessible. They tend to leave explicit instructions for their subordinates and others that work with them. These instructions often include when they will be accessible, when they check e-mail and voice mail, and when they will respond.

"People know that I do voice mail first thing in the morning and at the end of the day. If they need access to me in between times, they either have to call or come to see me (which I prefer anyway)."

These are the same people who leave very detailed messages on their voice mail telling callers where they are, when they will return, and when they will be checking messages. They also tend proactively to manage that process by informing clients and co-workers well in advance when their plans take them out of the office or away for an extended period of time.

The people who try to manage the expectations of others at work are generally sensitive to the expectations of their loved ones. These people consistently report that, when they are with their family, for example, they do not allow work to intrude. If they commit to a certain family activity, they also are committing to be accessible only to their family. This includes leaving cell phones and pagers at home and eliminating work-related interruptions.

"I always tell my clients well in advance (at least two weeks) if I'm going to be away on vacation or out of the country. And, I do the same for others I work with. I also try to check in just before I leave

to see if there are any last-minute issues. This seems to help a lot."

Some of the solutions being used by our contributors to limit accessibility include the following:

***

NOTE: Periodically we include lists of suggestions provided by our contributors. These have been edited only to eliminate duplication. Some ideas are contradictory; we believe that different people will find value in different ideas. As you read through the suggestions and ideas included in this section, you'll note techniques and creative approaches that you might want to implement. Or you'll land on an incredible idea that you believe can make a real difference in your life. Either way, your mind will subtly whisper "Ah-ha!" We suggest that you not lose the "Ah-ha!"s as you move along in the book (especially since you'll have a chance to use them later in a planning exercise). Use the margins to mark those items that cause your brain to register an "Ah-ha!"

• Solution Suggestions

- *Never take an activated cell phone to an appointment.*
- *Turn off your cell phone.*

- *Don't give out your cell phone number. Use it only for outgoing calls.*
- *Screen calls using caller ID.*
- *Respond only to pager; don't respond to cell phone.*
- *Work from home.*
- *Block out time when you cannot and will not be interrupted.*
- *Don't carry a cell phone or pager.*
- *Don't use the cell phone after 6:00P.M.*
- *Limit the number of e-mail and voice mail accounts to one each for business and one each for personal.*
- *Don't take your cell phone with you when you are focusing on someone else (for example, when you are watching one of your children's events).*
- *Learn to say no.*
- *Hold certain times sacred. If you made a commitment for a social event, maintain that commitment.*
- *Plan properly.*
- *Use the "delete" button early and often.*
- *Get my staff to call me only in an emergency.*
- *Make sure I am clear on what I value and what is important to me.*
- *Use only one technology tool when you're on your personal time.*
- *Forward your phone to voice mail.*
- *On your voice mail greeting, be clear about when you will and will not be available. Update that message regularly.*

- *Exercise to burn off stress.* (While this suggestion appears elsewhere, our contributors are quite clear in saying they also exercise *without* access.)
- *Maintain your commitment to work-free vacations.*
- *Create hours and days where you absolutely will not work or respond to work and hold those times sacred.*
- *Do voice mail first. The higher-priority items tend to come through on voice mail.*
- *Make your home phone number unlisted.*

***

Unless we can find some way to keep our sights on tomorrow, we cannot expect to be in touch with today.

—Dean Rusk

5

Unplug to Reenergize

When was the last time you completely left work behind? How frequently do you take work home, check e-mail or voice mail from home, or take your work with you on vacation? Do you feel you can't afford to *not* do these things?

> *"I had no strategy until I had a baby—a screaming or sleeping child will completely disconnect you!"*

The work many of us do is extremely demanding of both our time and energy. In many cases, you may allow the intrusion and justify the cost on a personal level for real or anticipated gains on the career level. To the extent that these choices are made consciously, based on enlightened awareness and endorsed by those who are also impacted, they may be reasonable for your particular circumstances and goals.

All too often, however, people come to realize that the trade-offs are not rational, and they yearn for an occasional and healthy separation from work. The ability to do this requires a combination of commitment and support that sometimes causes difficulty. Why? Isn't it simply a Just Do It mindset? Well, no.

Unfortunately, it's not so easy for everyone. For one thing, the ability to achieve separation suffers from a form of atrophy if not exercised routinely. For another, physical separation on a short-term basis does not elicit the benefit to be gained from a true separation over a longer period of time.

In reality, both types of separation are necessary. There's a growing body of literature—along with mounds of corroborating data from our research—supporting our premise that:

> *"I just got back from eight days in Hawaii, the first real vacation I've taken in three years. My wife and I have done a few five-day weekends, but I now realize that to get away I've really got to get AWAY, far away. When I'm at home, it is very difficult to completely disconnect. Still, setting non-work goals can help. I know that to shift focus away from work, I need something to shift my focus to. Having something else that is relatively consuming to throw my energy into is the only way I know how to get my head out of it."*

- Short intervals of separation (a.k.a. relaxation, disconnecting, meditation, mini-breaks, catnaps) throughout each day are necessary and valuable.
- Longer periods of separation involving a real and extended disconnect from work are essential over the long haul.

Our survey data suggest that people use a variety of tactics to separate themselves from work so they can create time and space to recharge. People have also reported creative ways they've learned to prevent work from invading personal time. Let's look first at effective techniques for taking short breaks throughout your workday to rest, relax, and reenergize, as well as at solutions for maintaining a sense of balance in your day:

> *"I get away. I go someplace where there are no phones and no computers and no e-mail and no inclination to use or find them."*

Daily Time-Outs

- *Take naps.*
- *Let people know your limits of accessibility and when calls will be returned.*
- *Spend time with pets.*
- *Exercise or engage in other physical activity.*

> *"On my desk are two large cards. Printedo n one is the word SMILE. On the other BREATHE. Every time I glance at each, I do each. I just can't help it. It does wonders for my physical and mental health!"*

- *Stop for decompression several times throughout the day.*
- *Turn off your pager and cell phone.*

The Siesta Solution

According to William and Camille Anthony, authors of *The Art of Napping at Work* (1999), people would benefit greatly from a few good naps. Who would argue with their premise that more than 50 percent of us are sleep-deprived? Noting that sleep deprivation is the second leading cause of automobile accidents, the Anthonys contend that workplace productivity is suffering as well. They suggest that workers are not just sleep-deprived, they are "nap ready," and employers would be wise to encourage workers to utilize workplace napping, a no-cost way to increase productivity.

***

- *Don't have a computer connection from home.*
- *Listen to opera during the commute to and from work.*
- *Create daily rituals (teatime, meditation, prayer, exercise).*
- *Don't answer the phone between 5:30 and 9:00P.M.*
- *Leave the office! Don't take work home!*

Here are other ways people achieve a sense of balance in their daily lives:

- *Always go out to lunch—sometimes with friends, sometimes with business associates.*
- *Never go out with business associates who talk business at lunch. Make it a time to decompress and de-stress.*
- *Take yoga lessons to learn controlled breathing and do that whenever I feel compressed—physically or emotionally.*

20 Minutes a Day Keeps the Doctor Away

There is growing evidence that 20 minutes a day is a critical figure for maintaining optimal mental health (www.accenthealth.com). Whether you are meditating, using the relaxation response, or simply taking time to sit with no interruptions and no noise, a number of experts consider 20 minutes a day to be the critical amount of time. Evidence shows that affording yourself this time each day slows the heart rate and breathing, lowers blood pressure, and relieves muscle tension.

You may choose a meditation or relaxation protocol, or simply sit quietly. At a minimum, find 20 minutes each day to surround yourself with uninterrupted silence. For that time (which in the opinion of some experts, doesn't need to be 20 consecutive minutes), just sit quietly with yourself ... breathe ... don't think.

***

- *Make definite plans for after-work hours that force me to leave work.*
- *Give myself a personal reading goal so I am not always working.*
- *Meditation; exercise; writing poetry as a release; reflection to provide perspective; remembering not to take myself too seriously.*
- *One half-hour of totally silent meditation each morning within 15 minutes of awakening. Keep a sanity daily to-do list (combination of most important personal and business items for each day). Review this list 2 to 3 times each day.*
- *Ensure that I have enough time for rest and recovery built into my schedule.*

Beyond daily efforts to maintain balance, focus, and energy, many people are beginning to appreciate the value of "mini-sabbaticals"—longer periods of time focused on nonwork activities, interests, or endeavors. It's becoming clear that mini-sabbaticals are somewhat like sleep, in that a 7-hour period of sleep affords us much greater restorative value than seven 1-hour segments within a 24-hour period. While daily time-outs positively impact productivity and are unquestionably vital, mini-sabbaticals provide the essential disconnect opportunity that involves the element of extended time.

Some people take weekly mini-sabbaticals and devote that block of nonwork time to family, educational, recreational, or religious activities. More people now recognize that, in addition to a significant break during the week, substantive breaks throughout the year are also essential.

We asked survey respondents to share strategies and techniques they use to unwind, reenergize, and renew their spirit. When considering the best solutions for your needs and circumstances, consider these mini-sabbatical techniques used by others:

Travel

- *Fun trips several times a year*
- *Travel for pleasure, or work some pleasure into business travel*
- *During long car journeys, switch off cell phone and listen to music*
- *Weekend trips*
- *Long drives*
- *A weekend away from everyone and everything*
- *Read only fun books/magazines on airplanes*

Time with Family and Friends

- *Participate in kids' activities without taking cell phone or work along*
- *Play with the kids*
- *Play cards or games*
- *Read aloud to children*
- *Spend time with friends who are not work associates*

- *Go to the park with kids*
- *Pray with kids and sing silly songs*
- *Seek out calm individuals*
- *Spend time with pets*
- *Write a letter (real pen/paper) to an old friend*

Nurture the Soul and Mind

- *Listen to music and take in the aromas of life*
- *Read*
- *Go to movies*
- *Attend conferences*
- *Go to the theater*
- *Attend religious services*
- *Enjoy ballet performances*
- *Meditate*
- *Go to the opera*
- *Write poetry*
- *Go to the hairdresser*
- *Practice yoga*
- *Take historical walking tours*
- *Do volunteering or community service*
- *Participate in religious groups and activities*
- *Browse through a bookstore*
- *Visit an art gallery*
- *Go someplace quiet and just sit*
- *Attend gatherings that are spiritual in nature*
- *Learn a new language*
- *Learn sign language*

Nourish the Body

- *Have therapeutic massage*
- *Do hard physical exercise (sweat a lot)*
- *Take up cycling*
- *Sleep*
- *Work out*
- *Train for the triathlon*
- *Go swimming*
- *Eat healthy*
- *Practice Tai Kwon Do*

Commune with Nature/Enjoy the Outdoors

- *Go sailing*
- *Go camping*
- *Take long walks in the woods*
- *Go fishing*
- *Go kayaking*
- *Go to the beach, the mountains, a lake house, a water park, or other places where access is difficult or impossible*
- *Go mountain biking*
- *Sit on the porch*
- *Go hiking*
- *Go bird watching*
- *Scuba diving*
- *Take the dog for a walk or a run in the park*
- *Go kite flying*

- *Take a minute each day to "notice" the outdoors (blue sky, sunset, leaves budding)*

> *"I am most restored when I am in nature, around other creatures and natural forces so that I'm able to experience myself as one of the whole, not in charge of the world."*

Hobbies

- *Play a musical instrument*
- *Play sports*
- *Do gardening*
- *Sing*
- *Explore your genealogy*
- *Cook*
- *Do woodworking*
- *Go racecar driving*
- *Take up photography*
- *Do crafts*
- *Go rock climbing*
- *Dance*
- *Do sewing or needlework*
- *Collect coins*
- *Collect stamps*
- *Go skating*
- *Take up painting and drawing*
- *Explore acting*
- *Make pottery*

- *Do quilting*

Aside from the techniques essential to unplugging and reenergizing, a number of overall strategies were reported that reflect an attitude or mindset integral to disconnecting:

- *Don't access technology during family activities.*
- *Just walk away from it.*
- *Do activities that don't require much cognitive attention.*
- *Don't carry a cell phone.*
- *Don't check voice mail.*
- *Don't check e-mail.*
- *Make a conscious decision not to work.*
- *Go into a state of FLOW where all concept of time is lost.*
- *No work talk allowed while on personal time.*
- *Shut off the phone or route it to voice mail.*
- *Leave work at work.*

> *"During long overseas trips, I e-mail my family when possible. Additionally, I keep a tape-recorded diary to give to them upon my return. This helps me feel connected during my journey, and allows them to share a bit of my trip (and my soul)."*

- *Avoid discussing work during family time.*
- *Stay out of my home office on the weekend.*
- *Do nothing at all.*
- *Laugh often.*

- *Stop and enjoy the view—literally and honestly.*
- *Have solitary time on weekends.*

In spite of the positive direction in which many people are moving to protect their personal lives, sanity, and personal commitments, a significant number of our research responses point to a drastic measure—The Extreme Disconnect—as an essential way to truly disconnect from work. Short of a drastic, remote, or extended alternative, it is clearly very difficult for some people to detach to the degree that they feel truly relaxed or refreshed. Hence, options such as the following are examples of The Extreme Disconnect:

> *"I don't have any effective strategies for balance in my life. In fact, my work time commitment has expanded to such an extent that personal time is secondary to work time. To completely disconnect, I **must** go out of the country!"*

- *Leave the country.*
- *Scuba dive in remote locations.*
- *Take a vacation where accessibility is difficult (cruise, hike in Death Valley, explore Idaho's river canyons).*
- *Leave town without beeper, cell phone, or laptop.*
- *Limit my network of friends to include very few work associates; avoid mixing business with pleasure.*

- *Take one week a year at a remote church camp in Northern Michigan with my entire family—unreachable for 8 days!*
- *Two-week vacation every year where access is impossible.*
- *Live in the country.*

Some words of wisdom are timeless and offer fundamental suggestions for balance, good health, and sanity. Recall whichever of the lessons your Mother preached:

- *You can't burn the candle at both ends.*
- *You can't have your cake and eat it too.*
- *All work and no play makes for a dreary day.*
- *Take time to smell the flowers.*
- *[Insert your own!]* _____

It's amazing how such words of wisdom prove to be truer than you could have imagined. In our effort to function in an increasingly wired world, it's critical to remember that without the proper physical, intellectual, and emotional rest, our bodies and minds cannot serve us to their full capacity. This damage, along with the damage done to relationships along the way, is rarely justified by the end results.

***

Take time to work
It is the price of success
Take time to think
It is the source of power

Take time to play
It is the secret of perpetual youth
Take time to read
It is the fountain of wisdom
Take time to be friendly
It is the road to happiness
Take time to share
Life is too short to be selfish
Take time to laugh
Laughter is the music of the soul
Take time to love and be loved
It is the privilege of the gods

—Anonymous

6

Techno–Triage

Through a variety of movies and television programs, you may be familiar with the medical version of triage. Simply put, *triage* is the sorting of casualties in terms of criticality and urgency and, in the process, putting aside those who can't be saved. While that approach to making decisions may seem callous, in reality that is what is required in times of great urgency, crisis, or overload. When you are making quick decisions in the midst of a frenzied work environment, you have to sort, scan, and filter as quickly as possible or run the risk of falling impossibly behind. If you don't do that, you also run the risk of focusing on the non-critical events in your life rather than those actions and activities that make a difference.

> *"You can't stop it—you can only hope to contain it."*

Earlier we discussed limiting access and disconnecting as ways of maintaining sanity. But, no matter how hard you try, information is still going to pour in. How you handle the information and messages that get through during "on" times is just as important as your ability to create "off" times, when information doesn't get through or you are inaccessible.

Our research clearly identifies a need to filter information, regardless of the form in which it comes to you. From very simple visual scanning to high-tech solutions, almost everyone we surveyed mentioned the absolute necessity of scanning, in some way, what comes to them. This allows them to focus on critical information and offers the opportunity to delete the extraneous. *Delete* is the operative word here, as most respondents either take action on a message or hit the delete key.

"Voice mail and e-mail can be a curse and a blessing at the same time. They are both because it is so easy to send and receive information. Attachments and e-mail links can increase the volume of information transferred tenfold. Managing e-mail requires a major allocation of time that was previously not required."

How people handle techno-triage, or where they apply their triage efforts, seems to relate in large part to their preferred mode of communication. Those who tend to focus on telephone or voice communication handle voice mail first. Those who are primarily tethered to e-mail find scanning techniques applicable to e-mail. While there is certainly overlap between the two mediums, and there are users who live in both worlds, distinctions between the two do exist.

> *"I determine my preferred method of communicating and let others know which channel will get the quickest response from me. This leverages my preferred channel."*

The Voice-Focused

There is a distinct group that is voice-centric. That is, they tend to place more emphasis on voice-to-voice communication, on the assumption that if someone—a customer, subordinate, or associate—took the time to call, it must be important. As a consequence, this group tends to place its focus on techniques that allow them to scan and filter voice mail messages. Our contributors explain some of the reasons for this preference with comments such as:

- *Voice mail is usually time-sensitive.*
- *I check voice mail first because that is where customers go.*
- *I figure if it's important enough for you to call me, I should return your call before the end of the business day.*

It appears that some of this is also a function of the organizational culture within which a person works. Some cultures *are* voice-to-voice oriented, while others are oriented to other mediums.

Does this group do anything particularly different from those that are e-mail focused? No. They do, however, clearly go first to voice mail, use it as their medium of choice and, more often than not, prefer to receive communication via the telephone or in person.

Filtering Voice Mail

How do people filter voice mail messages? The simple answer involves prioritizing, scanning, and deleting. Our contributors report that they respond to voice mail based on their priorities, quickly scanning to determine if the messages match their priorities and taking action by either responding or deleting as appropriate.

More specifically, our research responses included the following suggestions regarding voice mail:

- *I check messages often to avoid being hit with a large number all at once.*
- *I scan messages and answer only the important ones.*
- *I try to delegate, forwarding voice mail to others and encouraging them to take action.*
- *Just stay on top of it. You get to know after a while what you need to know and respond to. If someone really wants your opinion, they'll track you down until they get what they need.*
- *I do not do voice mail. Responding takes three times as long. Otherwise, my real work would come to a standstill.*

- *Be sure to clean out old messages at the end of each week.*
- *Use the delete key often.*
- *I process it in the early A.M. of each day only.*

On a related note, it is quite clear that a lot of people talk about setting expectations as a way of managing voice mail. Implicit here is the importance of managing your outbound messages as a way of setting expectations for those who are sending you messages or replies. This means that *you need to change your outbound message daily,* and you need to indicate when you will be checking messages and responding. While many people do this while on vacation or otherwise inaccessible, it is critical that this be done regularly if you want to manage expectations.

What Goes Around Comes Around

It was interesting to observe, throughout our data gathering about how people manage e-mail and voice mail, that we kept hearing echoes of the past. Specifically, as people describe their use of high-tech tools, they consistently use language reminiscent of the paper in-basket era. When in-baskets were overflowing, there was a clear emphasis on speed, and although it was rarely mentioned specifically, the real implication was on speed-reading. Just as clearly, the issues that apply to the "paper" world also apply to the "paperless" new world, with the possible exception that keyboard skills are now a factor in efficient processing of in-baskets. Likewise, some of the old maxims like "touch every item only once," still apply to new technologies.

Filtering e-Mail

e-Mail is a different animal. Not only does it require the same filtering skills as voice mail but achieving success with it requires an additional level of technical aptitude. The term *aptitude* is used deliberately because most e-mail systems provide the opportunity for the system itself to serve as a filter. Unfortunately, it seems that many people don't use this capability, thus adding to their e-mail burden. Also, due to its nature, e-mail allows more messages from multiple sources to enter your mailbox, and it is difficult to stop them.

How people handle e-mail varies widely. While suggestions appear below, bear in mind there are a variety of e-mail systems in use. Not all suggestions will be applicable to all systems. Know your system and its capabilities. Some of the techniques and suggestions detailed in the research responses include:

> *"You need to deal with it every day. I get on average 50 incoming messages every day via various contact points. I have learned to deal with what I can and ignore the rest. If a deadline is too tight, I send a one-line note back stating when I will be in a position to reply."*

- *Check e-mail and scan using scan function.*
- *With e-mail, I utilize a preferences option, which has been very helpful with prohibiting unwanted e-mail.*
- *File e-mail messages so they don't feel overwhelming.*
- *Turn off e-mail notification. Deal with mail first thing in morning and after lunch.*
- *Filter; don't respond immediately.*
- *Scan the e-mail and start with the last response to a string and delete all the interim messages.*
- *Avoid list serves. Use the filtering facility in good e-mail software and understand that all communications do not require an answer.*

Typhoid Mary

Our research reveals that many people work very hard at filtering and responding to messages. It's also clear that some people are "carriers" of message overload. They're the ones who remind us of the old adage "So-and-so doesn't have an ulcer but he/she causes them." More than a few of our respondents mentioned that they save all their outgoing messages and send them at the end of the day, or just before leaving the office. It occurs to us that these are the people who cause others to check their messages at night or feel overwhelmed first thing in the morning.

***

- *Delete unidentified e-mail without opening.*
- *Filter the information flow by sender and topic.*
- *When receiving multiple e-mails from the same person, open the most recent first and work backward.*

Above all else, the basics still remain. To be successful in surviving a blizzard of e-mail, you have to know what is important to you and act on it efficiently. How you use e-mail is still a choice based on your desire to control your world or be controlled by it.

Survival Tips for the e-Communication Culture

Earlier we discussed the establishment of an e-communication culture (norms, procedures) from an organizational perspective. One of the interesting things about asking people how they handle massive amounts of information is that you gain useful insight on how to get your message heard when you are the sender. What follows is a series of tips for your use when sending a message—either voice or e-mail:

- *Be brief.*
- *Clearly state the purpose of your message in the first 10 seconds or two sentences. Time and time again, people told us they make the*

decision to read, listen to, or delete a message in that timeframe. Contributors also reported relying on the subject or reference line in e-mails to make "read or delete" decisions.

- *Know what is important to the receiver. If you send a message that you think is important without regard for the receiver's interests, it is likely to be deleted (unless you happen to be the boss).*
- *Reply to e-mail with one-word responses when possible. Examples: agreed; discuss; fine; proceed; yes; ok; wait.*
- *Know when your key associates read e-mail or listen to voice mail. Most of our respondents set aside specific times for these two activities. Knowing this about your associates may make you more successful in managing the electronic clutter.*
- *Thou shalt not send copies to those who have no need.*

***

In today's world, triage is an essential survival skill. Without the ability *and* commitment to focus on what's critical and filter information based on that, you run the risk of being buried in an avalanche of messages and information.

Research responses included additional suggestions on the sorting of voice mail and e-mail messages:

- *Clean out your messages at least weekly. There's nothing worse than continuing to see messages accumulate.*
- *Stay current. Use evenings.*
- *The delete button is a great invention.*
- *Return messages at the end of the day.*
- *Prioritizing is the critical strategy. You need to communicate your priorities to those around you.*
- *Check each medium at least three times a day.*
- *I just try to keep up with it and not let it get out of hand. I travel with a computer so I don't fall behind when I'm on the road.*
- *Set aside regular times to answer them and don't get distracted.*
- *I decide whether it is essential to my mission, my job or my well-being. If not, I ignore it.*
- *Be disciplined, prioritize, and stay focused on the task at hand. Learn to say no.*
- *Screen messages and handle what you can each day for a scheduled period of time.*
- *I don't try to do it all. I prioritize who I need to communicate with and why. Sometimes I just let stuff go and figure when I need it, I'll find it.*

***

Technology is so much fun, but we can drown in our technology. The fog of information can drive out knowledge.

—Daniel J. Boorstin

7

Creating Community

There is a common thread to our discussions of Overload. Specifically, when Overload exists—in whatever form—it interferes with our ability to interact with the people around us in a truly human way. While there may be varying understandings of what it means to interact with others, no one disputes its importance in our lives. How each of us connects with one another to share love, joy, and a host of other emotions defines us as human beings.

The connections we have with others create a richness in our lives for which there is no substitute. Our contributors suggest consistently that being connected to others and being engaged in a community are synonymous. Technology, overwork, the desire to be rich, and a variety of other dynamics in our society often conspire to work against the fabric of togetherness toward which many of us strive. This chapter explores, with a wealth of wisdom from our contributors, ways of staying connected to others and strengthening community in our increasingly wired world.

There's a strong sense among those people we surveyed that the role of community in their lives is more and more important. *Community* is expressed, throughout our research responses, as active involvement in one-on-one relationships, connection with others in small groups, and contributions to others in a variety of forms and on numerous levels. For many of our contributors, community also embraces the sense of connection to a higher power.

When gathering input and success stories, we requested examples and techniques for maintaining a "sense of community and real human contact." Hence, responses included strategies for involvement at both a broad community level and a personal, individual level where intimate and lasting relationships are of primary importance.

While some people admit that available time and energy make involvement difficult, virtually everyone acknowledges that participation in a community is important and desirable. Many describe their community activities and personal relationships as vital to their sense of balance and of utmost importance in their lives. However, many people truly struggle to devote time to their community and human priorities. This is supported by recent studies, which indicate a decline in time available for friends, family, and socializing. This trend is associated not only with increased work but also with increased time devoted to computer use.

"Each day I leave and eat lunch outside the office, usually someplace quiet and with cloth napkins. It's my rule never to eat alone and always to pick

up the tab. I believe that outside of marriage there is little human contact as intimate as sharing a meal with someone in a quiet place."

Of course, technology offers us numerous ways to leverage its benefits for greater connectedness and participation in many new forms of online communities. It's not surprising to hear people extol the benefits of e-mail, online conferencing, and cell phones for maintaining contact with others. Indeed, e-mail has probably replaced handwritten letters as the preferred method of communication among families whose children are away at college or camp, whose grandparents are retired to a sunny location, or whose extended family members are now known as a result of genealogy searches conducted on the Web.

Many people appreciate the value of technology for expanding communication opportunities and, in some cases, creating communities for involvement. However, as our contributors expressed in various ways, and as Adam Goodheart wrote *(USA Today,* July 26, 2000): "Connectivity is not the same thing as connection."

The Broader Community

While a growing number of us struggle with the time and energy challenges inherent in the desire for authentic human and community connections, there is general acknowledgement of the vital role these relationships play in our lives. Aside from family relationships and personal relationships with close friends, an active life in community with others can involve:

- Volunteer activities and community service
- Networking proactively with friends, colleagues, work associates, or industry associates
- Leveraging skills and talents to serve on boards or in leadership positions in community, professional, or social organizations
- Involvement in religious or spiritual groups

It's clear that most people have limited time and are selective about how they share in broader communities. However, there's no shortage of the ways in which people experience and benefit from a community life:

- *I spend a lot of time on the telephone with clients and most of my important friendships have started from these groups. We have a lot in common and understand each others' priorities.*
- *Associating with others, getting involved with community issues, serving on boards whose purposes are to educate and/or to help others.*
- *I used to work on a number of volunteer boards and really miss it since my business has grown so fast. I'm hoping to rejoin and participate in the community next year. It's very important to me as part of the balance between family, friends, work, and community.*
- *I am actively involved and on the board of several community organizations. I juggle my work life so*

I can accommodate these activities and give back to the community.

- *Lots of lunches with both friends and colleagues—although this usually takes advance planning.*
- *Work with groups of people who are not "business biased" and try to understand what they see as being valuable, whether it's cleaning up a stream, delivering food to shutins, or reading to kids. Placing yourself in environments that are somewhat foreign provides a certain level of personal discomfort, and the energy you use to overcome the discomfort and convert it into contribution is powerful.*
- *I'm very much involved in my church family. When you work together on the issues of life that reach to your soul, you become spiritually joined. That's the ultimate in real human contact.*

For a growing number of us who work remotely from coworkers, colleagues, friends, partners, and business associates, technology has become an effective enabler of communication, relationship building, support networks, and information sharing. People are connecting via the "virtual water cooler," and are learning new ways to build effective virtual relationships. Further, emerging technologies offer expanded opportunities and support for online communities that facilitate information sharing and increased productivity within work groups.

Some of the technology tools people use to experience and expand their sense of community include:

- Telephone

- e-Mail
- Online chats
- Online video conferences
- Threaded message boards/roundtables
- Online communities

> *"I have a network of friends across the country with whom I have a "virtual happy hour" once every week. We stop working for a half hour at 5 o'clock (give or take a couple of hours!), grab a glass of wine, and have a conference call. Often several of us are online at the same time."*

Spirituality

There is an old bromide, commonly attributed to a football coach, used when speaking with his players about life. He let them know that his priorities were "God, family, and football," although not always in that order. This coach's perspective is not unlike the struggle many people seem to have when seeking the appropriate balance for spirituality within their lives. It is quite clear from our research that spirituality *is* important to people.

For many of our contributors, there is no question that spirituality is a vital source of strength and perspective in managing the hectic nature of their lives. Some express their spirituality as a deep connection with their vision of God and, in many cases, through active participation in an organized religion. For others, spirituality means connection with a power greater than themselves in less traditional ways.

> *"When things seem to get out of whack, I go back to my fixed, long-term priorities: (1) God, (2) family, and (3) work. It's important to have co-workers with the same or similar priority set."*

It intrigued us that, throughout our survey responses, regardless of the question asked, many people described some form of spirituality as their way of coping with the pressures of life. Whether they were asked questions about degrees of Access Overload, Information Overload, or Work Overload, or how to best maintain community, many people reflected on their use of prayer, meditation, or simply connecting with others on a deeper level as a significant way of coping.

> *"Services at my place of worship are like nourishment for the soul. I leave feeling renewed, relaxed, and in touch with my spiritual side. Services with my family and friends repre-*

sent a clear demarcation between work and non-work."

The Importance of Ritual

One of the implicit issues that arose in our research was the importance of ritual in people's lives. While no one spoke directly about creating rituals as a way of providing structure in their world, a significant number of our contributors reported activities that have become rituals for them. Whether it's worshipping, shutting the office door for designated concentration time, or checking e-mail at specific times in the day, people ritualize certain aspects of their lives to provide some control over it.

We found the importance of this for ourselves as we wrote this book. We made a ritual out of stopping for dinner with our daughter. It was important for us to separate work from family, or it would have been easy to fall into the very traps about which we were writing.

***

Much has been written in the popular press and in other places regarding the rise of spirituality in our lives, and our research bears this out. While it takes multiple forms, a spiritual dimension is important and meaningful to people. For many, spirituality is a critical resource in their search for sanity in today's fast-paced, hectic world.

Family First—No Doubt About It!

While some of our research resulted in more questions than answers, this was certainly not true on the issue of family and the unquestioned importance of it in the lives of so many. It's clear that, for a significant majority of people, there is increasing awareness of the meaning family holds for them and their corresponding commitment in terms of time, focus, and energy. Happily, this is not described as a burden, except in rare cases where it is in some conflict with work demands. Rather, the commitment to family is most often characterized as a desire and choice, driven by a core value and a balanced perspective regarding what is truly important in "the grand cosmic scheme of things." It's important to acknowledge that how people define and experience *family* is diverse. For some, *family* embraces those beyond a nuclear family.

The depth of commitment and overwhelming value people expressed in describing the essential human connection derived from family was profound and moving. This is not to suggest that simply holding family in high esteem and as a key value in one's life resolves the balance dilemma. Our research responses reveal that most people are indeed challenged to find sufficient time for family. There is no question, however, that the primacy of family is undisputed, as evidenced by these insights and life lessons shared by our contributors:

- *I spend as much time as possible with my grand-children. It makes up for the time I did not spend with my own children because I was too busy making a life for myself.*
- *I am very close to my family and they are good at helping me realize when I am ignoring my needs and theirs. It's helpful as a reminder of what is really important.*
- *I have lived in Canada for 20 years. Neither my husband nor I have a single family member living in Canada. My lot are all in Scotland; and my husband's children and four grandchildren are all in the USA. Phone—that's the lifeline. I talk to my Scottish siblings almost every day. The e-mail activity is also fast and furious. On the basis that "You can't take it with you," I will also—at the drop of a hat—jump on an airplane to Scotland or to the United States to see my grandchildren. And lastly, I have a small circle of really, really close friends who are an extremely important part of the tapestry.*
- *Family is the most important thing, and I make sure I tell them, even though I work long hours. Someone told me that one of the key things I owe my kids is a happy mother. So, I make sure that I am doing rewarding work that gives me emotional room for them. I have a spouse that is my partner in this. Same with my nanny. Therefore, if my kids*

ever doubt my commitment to them, I am not in a position where I have someone at home telling them "Oh, you poor babies ... your mother is crazy."

- *I keep certain times during the week sacred for nonwork/family/personal use. Make the needs of my family my top priority—Family First. Work projects are temporary endeavors. Family is life long.*
- *I never lose sight of the fact that nothing is as important as family.*

Creating community is the most fundamentally human of all the activities and issues addressed in this book. It brings together the sense of spirit, the power of family, and the strength of personal relationships that is the lifeblood of our humanity.

> *"I look for the "light" or humanity in every person I encounter. My sense of community does not come from groups I belong to because of limited time. Rather, I view each individual as part of a "larger whole" of which I am also a part. I view everything in terms of karma, which keeps me connected and responsible for the effects I create. Most of my intense contact comes from a small circle of friends and relatives."*

Retreating to the roots of your soul truly is the way to congruence and harmony in your life in the midst of a world that cannot and will not slow down. Reaching out to touch those around us—whether literally or metaphorically—is a key to inner peace.

***

Our concern is not how to worship in the catacombs, but how to remain human in the skyscrapers.

—Abraham Joshua Herschel

Part Three

ACTION

Two hundred more pages of solutions, strategies, success stories, suggestions, techniques, and ideas would provide you with an expanded wealth of options for managing various forms of Overload you may be experiencing. However, an extended dissertation of such options won't matter one whit if there isn't the desire, intent, and decision on your part to take the action necessary to make meaningful changes in your life. Such change is generally not easy. But it seems the hardest part is the beginning—to take the first step.

Initial steps, processes and actions, and ultimate changes will be uniquely yours. There is not a "one size fits all" solution, nor is there a methodology or set of answers applicable to everyone. The only prevailing truth is the certainty that nothing will change until you decide that it will, and that only you can decide. Determining how to invest your life and energy each day is clearly a highly personal and extraordinarily important set of decisions.

Consider as you reflect on the choices that you've made or are making in your life:

- WHY have you made those choices?
- WHO are they impacting?
- WHAT, if anything, would you prefer be different?

- HOW can you take an initial step in making choices that are more congruent with your desires, vision, values, dreams, and passions?

Many people feel strongly that the way they're investing their time and energy fails to reflect their personal values and priorities. They see family as priority number one; place a high value on pursuing a spiritual path; consider volunteer activities integral to their contribution to society; believe in taking care of themselves through exercise, relaxation, hobbies, learning activities—if only they had the time! Interestingly, none of our contributors reported anyone holding a gun to their head to coerce the choices they have made!

In reality, self-imposed limits and demands are just that—self-inflicted restrictions to the degree of joy you can experience. Analyze the logic of any rationale you may have for the limitations of your life. Clear and honest thinking will ultimately lead to a likely conclusion: Every circumstance, limitation, opportunity, joy, and problem that exists in your life is there because of a choice you've made. This is certainly true with regard to the relationship, and the degree of balance, that exist between your work and your personal life.

***

Most people tend to drive into the future with their eyes on the rear-view mirror.

—Marshall McLuhan

8

Your Digital Divide

We've made a few assumptions about the readers of this book. Specifically, we believe the book is valuable to people in phases of their lives characterized by:

- Greater emphasis on introspection
- Increased conflict among priorities
- Elevated awareness of the search for deeper meaning
- Increased frustration with work demands that result in the deferral of true desires
- Expanded feelings of complete exhaustion and depletion

While people may differ in their experience of these dynamics dependent upon age, maturity, and experience, these factors are less significant than the way in which people become aware of and deal with the challenges that arise, whenever they occur. The timing of dissatisfactions in life may have more to do with the pace, demands, and type of work undertaken than with your chronological age. For example, there's increasing evidence of significant reevaluation and reconsideration of choices and tradeoffs by those who were swept up in the intensity of the dot com world. Those who found the personal costs and elusive payoff not worth the sacrifice represent a wide range of ages.

Any number of situations, circumstances, crises, significant emotional events, or evolving growth opportunities may allow the still small voice within finally to be heard: "Something is not right!" Whatever the precipitating circumstance or incident, people often reach a point where they describe feelings of being overworked, stressed out, bored with work and life, or out of balance.

The Illusion of Balance

A review of popular and business literature, as well as a survey of corporate values statements, reveals that work/life balance is a significant topic of interest and concern. From soccer moms to highly placed executives, more people are complaining about the lack of balance in their lives. To hear most of them discuss the topic, it sounds as if their lives are essentially out of control. This loss of control may be the result of overload. The dynamic can be exacerbated by the need to strive for perfection in all your endeavors. A constant juggling of the demands of work, personal life, family, and friends make it seem that our lives are out of control, subject to the whims and demands of others.

The image this evokes is one of chaos, with employees constantly reminding their employers about "quality of life," and workers complaining to one another about how busy they are. In truth, as we have noted elsewhere, people *are* busier than they have been before. But, if all the rhetoric is to be believed, it would seem to imply that most people are dysfunctional, wallowing in the morass of conflicting pressures in their daily lives.

We think the problem of lack of balance may actually be a myth—and here's why. In reality, little permission is given to talk about appropriate balance in your life. When, for example, was the last time you sat around at a party and talked about how "whole" and balanced you were feeling at that moment? It's rarely done. In some communities and social groups, there's a definite one-upsmanship associated with excessively busy schedules and limited opportunities for families to dine together (let alone spend quality time together!).

Likewise, while most organizations pay lip service to the value of a balanced life, their underground culture (or, in many cases, their explicit culture) contradicts that notion. How many organizations create heroes or heroines out of those individuals who go home at the end of the workday, are devoted to their spiritual endeavors, participate actively in the community, and are productive at work? The reality in most organizations is that the individuals who are lionized are the ones who seem to eat, sleep, and breathe the company.

Think about your own company or organization. Who is rewarded and recognized? The occasional annual report profiles an employee who seems to have a balanced life (although those profiled tend to be employees who represent the company well in the community). More often, the employees recognized are those who have achieved extraordinary results or gone the extra mile in pursuit of company goals. The clear message being sent to employees is—work hard, work long, and, above all, *talk about how busy you are.*

> *"I don't believe that an organization can help or hinder individuals in their search for personal peace. The achievement of harmony, happiness, balance, and contentment is not related to a person's circumstances or to their surroundings. Anyone who believes that their company can contribute to, or detract from, their sense of well-being is probably going to spend most of life without it. Peace comes from within, not from without."*

As a result, it has become almost socially incorrect to express satisfaction with the state of balance in your life. So, it becomes even more difficult for people to achieve balance when there's little offered in the way of support, encouragement, and positive models for the balanced lifestyle. In spite of the rhetoric, there's clearly an inherent association between perceived achievement levels and unbalanced lives as evidenced by insane schedules.

But only you live your life, and you will live with the consequences of your choices. Make no mistake about it, there *are* consequences and costs. Making congruent choices sometimes means making hard decisions that have long-term implications. The choice to spend more time with your family (and less at work) may alter your career path. Or, in the reverse case, the decision to focus on your career at the expense of family and friends may leave you alone with your career.

How you craft and live your life is a choice, albeit one that may not always be conscious. Creating a life characterized by congruence, balance, or integration is a personal choice driven by passion. Each of us makes these choices based on what we deem to be important. While you may moan about the lack of balance in your life or worry about how little time you spend with your family, the truth is, you've made choices. Don't misunderstand. We're not naïve; we fully recognize there are busy episodes in a work life or career during which sacrifices must be made. But, too many people allow those circumstances to control their lives without conscious thought. In some ways it's like the sixties' saying, "Not to decide is to decide" (Harvey Cox). Too many of us have allowed our situation to make decisions for us—and then sat back and complained about the choice.

Which brings us to the primary point of this book:

What Are Your Choices?

Based on the priorities and values you identified in Chapter 2, along with the examples of choices and solutions offered by others in Chapters 4 through 7, what changes, choices, and commitments are right for you? It's clear from the experiences and insights shared by our contributors that deferral of clear decisions based on individual values can lead to compromises that have long-term ramifications. These consequences may involve tradeoffs you will ultimately consider unreasonable.

The Path to Congruence

This leads to additional assumptions we made about our readers. If you've reached this point in the book, it's likely you:

- Experience the challenges associated with achieving a life of balance and serenity
- Are exploring solutions that are appropriate for you and your life circumstances
- Have decided to make or are seriously considering changes in your life that will lead you to a more balanced and congruent life

To this end, we offer a process to help as you move on the path toward greater balance, congruence, and fulfillment in your life. As depicted in *The Path to Congruence* on the next page and discussed in the earlier chapters of this book, attainment of congruence begins with clarification of values.

Without clear values, your actions and behaviors are driven by influences, demands, pressures, and expectations—both externally and internally generated—that may not help you reach the objectives that are consistent with your true desires and authentic

The Path to Congruence

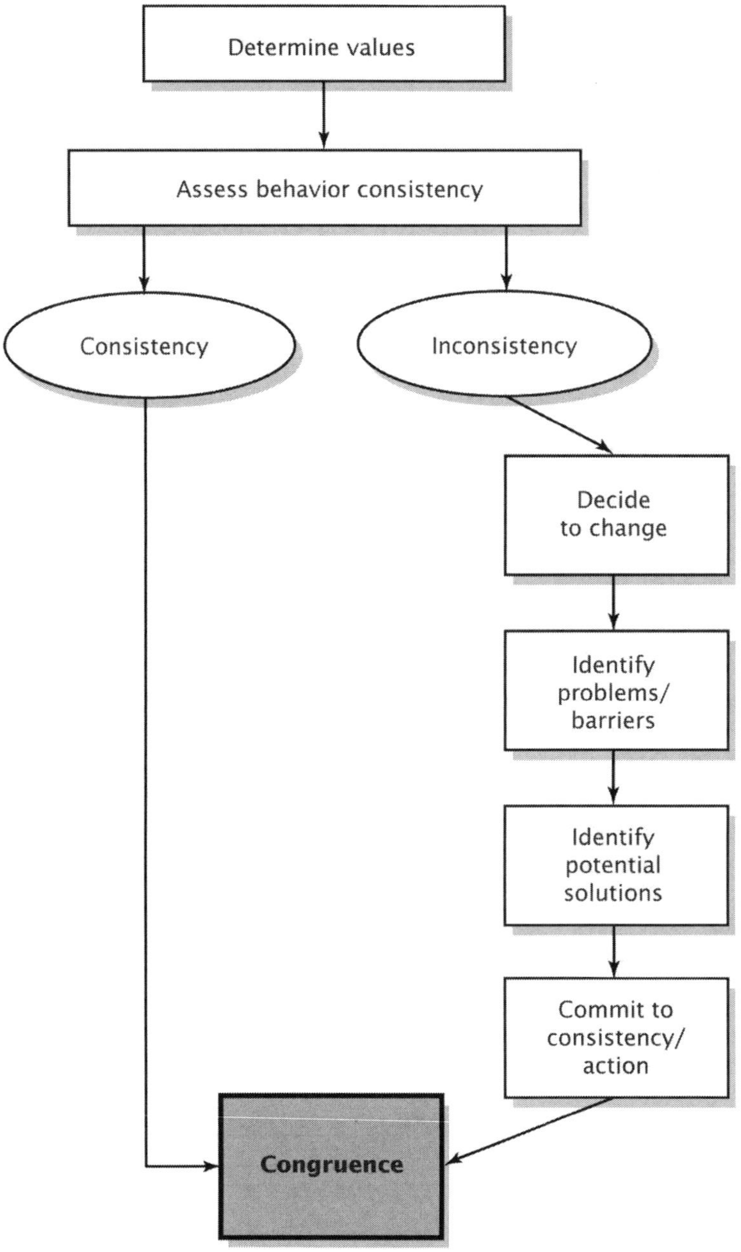

values. Too many people remain muddled about their values until they've compromised them or made tradeoffs from which they can no longer recover.

Clearly articulating your values, then honestly assessing your choices, behaviors, and actions in light of your values, is an essential component on your personal road to congruence. The exercises in Chapter 2 are designed to facilitate this process. If you found strong consistency between your values and your behavior, you are enjoying a congruent life.

If, however, you identify inconsistencies between your values and the choices you've made or the way you invest your time and energy, it's likely you are experiencing inner conflict. Indeed, much of the exasperation, angst, depression, and exhaustion associated with being out of balance is, in reality, a result of being incongruent. Moving beyond this state begins with the decision to make the necessary changes. You may not even know what the changes will entail. However, it's essential that you make a commitment on both a psychological and emotional level, and say to yourself:

Something Has Got to Change!

Now you are ready to begin!

Your Congruence Plan

We firmly believe that prescriptive processes and tools are inconsistent with the way adults learn or alter their behavior. Therefore, we have devised a process that supports, guides, and enables *your* choices and changes. This process will assist you in identifying problems and barriers, identifying potential solutions, and committing to consistent action. And here's the really good news: it's pretty simple! That's because about 90 percent of the result is driven by your decision and your commitment to make changes—and no one can do that for you.

So, let's begin. We suggest you note your responses on the next pages, create a separate document, make a poster, or commit your plan to writing in whatever other way makes it meaningful, visible, and workable for you.

As a reminder, your congruence plan is not etched in stone. Review it regularly—monitor your progress, discard ideas that aren't working, or try new techniques to meet new challenges.

My Congruence Plan

Using the information and insights you gathered from the questionnaires and exercises in Chapter 2, along with the "Ah-ha!"s you noted in Chapters 4 through 7, complete the following:

- Having noticed the lack of balance and congruence in my life, I want to make the following changes that will allow me to live a more congruent life:

[Space left intentionally blank in the original book]

Regarding the degree of Overload in my life, I want to make changes so my life and work are different in these ways (Consider how you experience Information Overload, Access Overload and Work Overload. Also consider the specific visible, measurable, and sustainable changes that support your values and goals.)

- The situations and barriers that contribute to my difficulties with balance and Overload include:

[Space left intentionally blank in the original book]

- Based on my values, the solutions offered in Chapter 4 through 7, my unique circumstances, and my capabilities, I choose to implement the following solutions in my life.

I will prioritize and organize my life and work more effectively by:

[Space left intentionally blank in the original book]

I will take daily time-outs by incorporating the following into my day:

[Space left intentionally blank in the original book]

I will take periodic breaks throughout the week, month and year and enjoy mini-sabbaticals in the following ways:

[Space left intentionally blank in the original book]

I will nurture my soul and mind by:

[Space left intentionally blank in the original book]

I will nourish my body and care for my physical wellbeing by:

[Space left intentionally blank in the original book]

My commitment to act on these changes will be clear, visible, and firm because of these steps I will take:

[Space left intentionally blank in the original book]

(Options may include a contract with yourself or others, a documented action plan, a monitoring plan checked periodically by you or a significant other, a commitment event, etc.)

Holiday Reflection: A Reminder of What Really Matters

All hell broke loose for me yesterday. I had so many crises going on that I could barely keep track of them. It is always difficult for me when I am out of the office. But yesterday I had to be at the office, at CNBC, for Squawk Box, at the Spy Bar to film a commercial for TheStreet.com , monitor my stocks—all of which were going down—and get this piece out.

At 2P.M. I was juggling two cell phones and my personal computer, while a woman put makeup on my face and a guy tied a tie around my neck. Suddenly, Jeff, my partner, says "Call your wife at home, there's a problem."

I call, and sure enough our daughter is sick and has to be rushed to the hospital. Dehydration.

I say to my wife that I'd love to help out but I've got 30 people waiting on me at the commercial site, and two companies begging for me to do several things at once. She says, "Okay. Do what you have to do." And I hang up.

And then it hits me. On Monday Bill Griffeth, the excellent anchor on CNBC, said he couldn't get the story about the Luby's chairman killing himself out of his head. Griffeth is usually so jocular and funny that we all stop and listen at my shop for his 1:55P.M. droll lesson of the day. But that day he talked about how important it was to remember that even if business is going poorly, it's just business. It will come back. It will sort itself out. And if it doesn't, there will be another opportunity. But family, life—now that's real.

I picked up the phone and called my wife back. I said I am stopping the shoot right now no matter how much it costs, jumping into my car and I will be there immediately.

Twenty minutes later I walked into the hospital and I could hear my daughter crying for her daddy all the way down the hall. I rushed in and she said, "Daddy, these people put this thing in my arm and it hurts, why didn't you stop them?" I explained to her that it was an IV, and she needed the energy from it. "But, Daddy," she asked, "Why didn't you get here sooner?"

I took a deep breath and said, "I got here as soon as I could." And for a moment, in all the turmoil, I felt good. I hadn't lied. I had gotten there as fast as I could.

Now it's 5:34A.M. My daughter slept well and is doing better already. I'm looking at my screens. I'll make it back. Things will be fine.

I did the right thing. Thanks Bill.

James J. Cramer, CEO
www.thestreet.com

9

Reminders—For Those Who Don't Own a Retrospectoscope

For many of the people we talked with and surveyed, there is a common thread—a prevailing message runs through their stories and perspectives. Many of us have heard the suggestion that no one on his or her deathbed ever worries about the overflowing in-basket that's being left behind or regrets not having spent more time at work before moving to the Great Beyond. Well, we're pleased to report that more people than you might suspect actually believe this *and* are working hard to apply its wisdom before it's too late.

The collective search for sanity and balance throughout our culture is gaining acceptance and momentum. Our society acknowledges the yearning within which our individual search is rooted; the validity of our desire to achieve sanity and congruence in our lives; and the elevated sense of urgency that characterizes our clamoring for calm.

The adage "Life is short" isn't likely to arouse much disagreement. On a micro level, people are frustrated by the brevity of each day—exacerbated by the overload of information, the demands of near-constant accessibility, and the oppression of unending volumes of work. On a macro level, the precious and tenuous reality of our existence is becoming increasingly apparent.

One of our contributors described the perspective he maintains in his interactions with others: "When I look at someone, I try to feel the fact that one day they will die."

And so shall we all.

Let us remember to live our lives abundantly ... take time for your priorities that, in the end, really matter ... take care of yourself and those you love, for you may not be with them tomorrow ... and choose wisely, for your choices define both the limits and possibilities of your life.

And when the small voice within quietly and persistently reminds you of the lack of order, focus, balance or congruence in your life, let your reply be:

I Can Change.

We urge you to reach out to touch the heavens, grab for the stars, find dimensions of your soul, embrace life and those around you.

And we remind you that your search for sanity in our increasingly wired and weary world is an evolving process, the unfolding journey of your life, a series of transitions and choices that lead you to stretches of congruence and calm, and to peaceful acceptance of your choices.

***

We live our lives forward but we understand them backward.

—Sören Kierkegaard

Special Afterword

"Little Baby Stary"

Once upon a time, there was a female star and a male star. they were married and had a child called Stary Jr. They were happy with what they had. The End

Jennimarie

Appendix

Contributors provided input to this book by completing the following questionnaire. The 200+questionnaires and interviews we gathered included an almost even distribution by gender and represented a wide range of positions, industries, and geography.

We are continuing our research and would value your contribution. This questionnaire is designed to gather information, examples, and techniques from people who face the challenge of balancing work and life demands. In particular, the impact technology has on the ability to achieve balance is being explored.

Feel free to copy the questionnaire and send it to us by fax or mail. You can also complete the questionnaire online by visiting www.dotcalmbook.com. We look forward to your contribution to our continuing research.

Fax

724.934.9348

Complete Online

www.dotcalmbook.com

Mail

ALLearnative
10592 Perry Hwy.,

Suite 201
Wexford, PA 15090 USA

Dot Calm Questionnaire

Name _____ Date _____

Current job/employer

[space left intentionally blank in the original book]

What percentage of time do you travel in connection with your job? _____%

Years in current job _____ Years in workplace (full-time) _____

Age: _ 20-30 _ 30-40 _ 40-50 _ 50-60 _ 60+

Telephone (_____) Fax (_____) _____

E-mail _____

Please provide 1 or 2 of your best techniques for how you:

Balance all the demands of your life and work?

[space left intentionally blank in the original book]

Limit your accessibility to avoid interruptions to personal time?

[space left intentionally blank in the original book]

Completely disconnect from work?

[space left intentionally blank in the original book]

Unwind, reenergize and renew your spirit/energy?

[space left intentionally blank in the original book]

Manage the barrage of e-mail, voice mail, and information that exists?

[space left intentionally blank in the original book]

Can we include your name on our list of contributors? _ Yes _ No

Thank you for your time, ideas and willingness to share your experience!

Related Reading

The Art of Napping at Work, by William and Camille Anthony (Larson Publishing, 1999)

Coming Up for Air, by Beth Sawi (Hyperion, 2000)

Daddy@Work, by Robert Wolgemuth (Zondervan Publishing House, 1999)

Finding Time, by Leslie A. Perlow (Cornell University Press, 1997)

The Future of Success, by Robert B. Reich (Knopf, 2001)

The Future of Work, by Charles Grantham (McGraw-Hill, 2000)

Harvard Business Review on Work and Life Balance (Harvard Business School Press, 2000)

The Heart Aroused, by David Whyte (Currency Paperback, 1996)

Lifebalance, by Linda Richard Eyre (Fireside Books, 1996)

The Overworked American, by Juliet B. Schor (Basic Books, 1993)

The Power of Purpose, by Richard J. Leider (Berrett-Koehler, 1997)

Simplicity: The New Competitive Advantage in a World of More, Better, Faster, by Bill Jensen (Perseus Books, 2000)

Take Back Your Time, by Jan Jasper (St. Martin's Griffin, 1999)

Take Time for Your Life, by Cheryl Richardson (Broadway Books, 1999)

Telecosm, by George Gilder (Free Press, 2000)

The Time Bind, by Arlie Russell Hochschild (Metropolitan Books, 1997)

Work & Family, by Sue Shellenbarger (Ballantine Publishing Group, 1999)

Work: Making a Living and Making a Life, by Joshua Halberstam, Ph.D. (Berkley Publishing Group, 2000)

The Working Life, by Joanne B. Ciulla (Times Books, 2000)

Contributors

The authors gratefully acknowledge the contributions of all those who participated in our research or added value in some other way. Those who agreed to have their name included in the book are listed here.

Y. Carol Asam
Christopher M. Avery
Dick Ayling
Neil D. Bassi
Helen Frank Bensimon
David Binder
Cindy Bird
Rick Blackstone
Diane Blecha
Kathy Bogacki
Jim Bolton
Vincent Borreli
Pat Bruns
Bob Buerger
Jim Bulger
Lee Ann Burr
Bill Byham
Dennis Campbell
Colin Chaplain
Tom Chase
Dan Chaverin
Debra Ciarrocchi

Gary Corba
Denise Corrales
Bill Corsini
Bruce Court
Jack Covert
James J. Cramer
Kelly Crofoot
Lynne Dardanell
Bob DeContreras
Linda Dinnocenzo
Michael Disabato
Andrea Dixon
Doug Dixon
Kris Downing
Marci Passos Duffy
Jim Dupree
Jody Ellis
Audrey Ellison
Tom Emerson
Hollis Engley
Ron Fetzer
Jean Findlater
Teryl Flynn
Brian Foley
Jason Gegg
Barbara Pate Glacel
Ann Goodson-Daley
Beverly A. Grant
Erica Groschler
Laura A. Grover

Ray Halagera
Richard S. Hamilton
John Hayden
Marcia Heath
Pat Heim
Diane Hessan
Sandy Hilker
David Huffner
Peggy Hutcheson
David Jones
Joanne Jorz
Beverly Kaye
Erica J. Keeps
David M. Kolb
James M. Kouzes
Don Kraft
Carmen Lasso
Darlene Lea
Allison Lee-Mann
Stewart Levine
Mark Levy
Glenn Lovelace
Gordon MacDonald
Michael Mariotti
Scott McCabe
Paul McCollough
Clark McGee
Timothy S. Mech
Nancy Michaels
Linda P. Miller

Bill Molloy
Richard Moore
Frank Napoli
Jennifer Ottino
Matt Paese
Anne Palmer
Steve Paskoff
Dave Patrick
Detta Penna
Alice Pescuric
Cynthia Uminski Pfoff
Steve Popovich
Doreen Price
Mike Ringuette
Victoria Risacher
Jane Rollman
Barry Rosen
Tamar Rosenfeld
Todd Rosenfeld
Bob Ruckel
Janet Ruckel
Susan C. Sargent
Chris Savikas
Jason Schlosser
Pam Schmidt
Tom Schott
Joan Schwetz
Darryl L. Sink
Jack Snader
Mark Steingold

Leslie Sturzenberger
Karla Swatek
Jennimarie Dinnocenzo Swegan
Sue Swegan
Lori Taylor
Pat Templeton
Mitchell Tenzer
Portia O. Ulinski
Dan Vargas
Shannon Rye Wall
Jim Walton
Jenny Warner
Chuck Weintraub
Steve Weitzenkorn
Rich Wellins
LaVerne Wentworth
Harriet West
Jane Whitmore
Stephanie Whittaker
Carol Willett
Roy H. Williams
Dwayne D. Woodruff
Jillian Woodruff
Luke Wyckoff
Steven Alex Zaharakos
David A. Zimmer

About the Authors

Debra A. Dinnocenzo and Richard B. Swegan

Debra Dinnocenzo and Rick Swegan have lived the issues described in *Dot Calm: The Search for Sanity in a Wired World,* throughout their marriage and partnership, long before they decided to write this book.

Debra is president of ALLearnatives®, a learning and development firm that consults with organizations to help implement alternative work strategies and remote work initiatives. Debra has more than twenty years experience in marketing, sales and product management. She has worked in executive positions for Development Dimensions International (DDI), Ridge Associates and Learning International, a division of Times Mirror. A graduate of Central Michigan University, Debra holds an M.A. and B.S. in business. In addition to publishing numerous articles, she is also the author of *101 Tips for Telecommuters* (Berrett-Koehler, 1999). In her spare time, Debra enjoys walking in the woods near her home, writing poetry, and spending time with her daughter Jennimarie.

Rick Swegan currently serves as global account manager for Development Dimensions International (DDI), where he manages the firm's relationship with its largest global client. He is DDI's career sales revenue leader and has been awarded top sales honors for nine consecutive years. Prior to his tenure at DDI, Rick was vice president of human resources for a fast food chain and held administrative positions at several colleges and universities. He received his B.A. from The College of Wooster and an M.Ed. from Ohio University. Rick is a voracious reader and collector of books—he still has all the books he ever owned and especially enjoys collecting juvenile books. In addition to spending time with his daughters, he enjoys exploring his family history (which he's traced back ten generations) and serves as a partner in ALLearnatives.®

Rick and Debra work from their home office in Wexford, Pennsylvania where they have seven phone lines, a home computer network, wonderful views of the forest, and frequent visits by flocks of wild turkey and herds of whitetail deer. They enjoy life together with their daughter, Jennimarie, and their cat, Vincent.

More Information

If you're interested in:

- Ordering additional copies of this book
- Downloadable versions of the questionnaires and exercises used throughout this book
- Additional information and resources related to topics addressed in this book
- Scheduling a ***Dot Calm*** seminar, presentation, or keynote address
- Participating in continuing research on overload and balance
- Sharing a personal story related to the topics contained in ***Dot Calm*** for future publication

Please visit our website: www.dotcalmbook.com

You can also reach us at:

*E-mail:*info@allearnatives.com

Telephone: 724.934.9349

Fax: 724.934.9348

Address: ALLearnatives®

10592 Perry Highway, Suite 201

Wexford, PA 15090 USA

Berrett-Koehler Publishers

BERRETT-KOEHLER is an independent publisher of books, periodicals, and other publications at the leading edge of new thinking and innovative practice on work, business, management, leadership, stewardship, career development, human resources, entrepreneurship, and global sustainability.

Since the company's founding in 1992, we have been committed to supporting the movement toward a more enlightened world of work by publishing books, periodicals, and other publications that help us to integrate our values with our work and work lives, and to create more humane and effective organizations.

We have chosen to focus on the areas of work, business, and organizations, because these are central elements in many people's lives today. Furthermore, the work world is going through tumultuous changes, from the decline of job security to the rise of new structures for organizing people and work. We believe that change is needed at all levels—individual, organizational, community, and global—and our publications address each of these levels.

We seek to create new lenses for understanding organizations, to legitimize topics that people care deeply about but that current business orthodoxy censors or considers secondary to bottom-line concerns, and to uncover new meaning, means, and ends for our work and work lives.

Also by Debra A. Dinnocenzo

- A concise, user-friendly guide for telecommuters, written by a veteran telecommuting executive with more than a decade of first-hand experience as both a telecommuter and telemanager.
- Full of immensely helpful advice in bite-sized and easily implementable pieces.
- Focused on the myriad tasks and roles telecommuters must handle on a daily basis, from managing their own time to dealing with family distractions, from working with other team members and clients to using technology efficiently and well.
- Includes a Telecommuter Self-Assessment Checklist so readers can determine if telecommuting is right for them, a Telecommuter Start-Up Guide, and a Telecommuter Resource Guide to refer to whenever telecommuting gets tough.

- The perfect guide for anyone who wants to succeed in this exciting and challenging new way to work.

Available at your favorite bookstore or at www.TipsForTelecommuters.com

VIDEOS ALSO AVAILABLE!

Dot Calm

The Search for Sanity in a Wired World

Offering solutions for the overconnected, overworked, overinformed, and overwhelmed!

Bridging the Distance

Virtual Teams on the Road to Results

A 17-minute video program based on Debra Dinnocenzo's highly praised book, *101 Tips for Telecommuters.* The video combines an overview of key learning points with a dramatic case study. See a virtual team learn using the seven skills necessary for virtual team success.

For additional information or to purchase or preview videos, please contact:

Spread the Word!

Berrett-Koehler books and audios are available at quantity discounts for orders of 10 or more copies.

Dot Calm

The Search for Sanity in a Wired World
Debra A. Dinnocenzo and Richard B. Swegan

To find out about discounts on orders of 10 or more copies for individuals, corporations, institutions, and organizations, please call us toll-free at (800)929-2929.

To find out about our discount programs for resellers, please contact our Special Sales department at (415)288-0260; Fax: (415)362-2512. Or email us at bkpub@bkpub.com.

Berrett-Koehler Publishers
PO Box 565, Williston, VT 05495-9900
Call toll-free! **800-929-2929** 7 am-12 midnight
Or fax your order to 802-864-7627
For fastest service order online: **www.bkconnection.com**

M

N

O

P

Q

R

S

T

Books For ALL Kinds of Readers

At ReadHowYouWant we understand that one size does not fit all types of readers. Our innovative, patent pending technology allows us to design new formats to make reading easier and more enjoyable for you. This helps improve your speed of reading and your comprehension. Our EasyRead printed books have been optimized to improve word recognition, ease eye tracking by adjusting word and line spacing as well as minimizing hyphenation. Our EasyRead SuperLarge editions have been developed to make reading easier and more accessible for vision-impaired readers. We offer Braille and DAISY formats of our books and all popular E-Book formats.

Printed in Dunstable, United Kingdom

91223535R00100